CIMA

Operational Level

E1

Managing Finance in a Digital World

Exam Practice Kit

For exams from January 2023

Ninth edition 2022

ISBN 9781 0355 0276 9
e-ISBN 9781 0355 0327 8

British Library Cataloguing-in-Publication Data
A catalogue record for this book
is available from the British Library

Published by

BPP Learning Media Ltd
BPP House, Aldine Place, 142/144 Uxbridge Road
London W12 8AA

www.bpp.com/learningmedia

Printed in the United Kingdom

Your learning materials, published by BPP Learning Media Ltd, are printed on paper obtained from traceable, sustainable sources.

We are grateful to the Chartered Institute of Management Accountants for allowing us to reproduce extracts from the CIMA exam blueprint. An up-to-date version of the full blueprint is available at www.cimaglobal.com/examblueprints.

Contents

Questions and answers

Practice mock

Question and Answer index

Using your BPP Exam Practice Kit

One of the key criteria for achieving exam success is question practice. There is generally a direct correlation between candidates who study all topics and practise exam questions and those who are successful in their real exams. This Kit gives you ample opportunity for such practice throughout your preparations for your OT exam.

All questions in your exam are compulsory and all the component learning outcomes will be examined so you must **study the whole syllabus**. Selective studying will limit the number of questions you can answer and hence reduce your chances of passing. It is better to go into the exam knowing a reasonable amount about most of the syllabus rather than concentrating on a few topics to the exclusion of the rest.

Practising as many exam-style questions as possible will be the key to passing this exam. You must do questions under **timed conditions**.

Breadth of question coverage

Questions will cover the whole of the syllabus so you must study all the topics in the syllabus.

The weightings in the table below indicate the approximate proportion of study time you should spend on each topic, and is related to the number of questions per syllabus area in the exam.

E1 Managing Finance in a Digital World Syllabus topics	Weighting
A Role of the finance function	20%
B Technology in a digital world	20%
C Data and Information in a digital world	20%
D Shape and structure of the finance function	20%
E Finance interacting with the organisation	20%

(CIMA exam blueprint, 2023/2024)

Blueprint Index

Listed below are the lead syllabus outcomes and component outcomes from the CIMA official Blueprint along with the numbers of the questions (excluding the mock exams) covering those topics. If you need to concentrate your practice and revision on certain topics, or if you want to attempt all available questions that refer to a particular component outcome, you will find this index useful.

Lead outcome	Component outcome	Questions	Completed
A1 The roles of the finance function in organisations	a Enables organisations to create and preserve value	1.3, 1.4, 1.5, 1.7, 1.10, 1.12, 1.13	
	b Shapes how organisations create and preserve value	1.2, 1.15, 1.19	
	c Narrates how organisations create and preserve value	1.1, 1.6, 1.8, 1.9, 1.11, 1.14, 1.16, 1.17, 1.18, 1.20	

BPP LEARNING MEDIA

Lead outcome	Component outcome	Questions	Completed
A2 The activities that finance professionals perform to fulfil the roles	a Collates data to prepare information about organisations	2.3, 2.4, 2.7, 2.15	
	b Provides insight to users by analysing information	2.8, 2.9	
	c Communicates insight to influence users	2.1, 2.5, 2.6, 2.10, 2.11	
	d Supports the implementation of decisions to achieve the desired impact	2.2, 2.14	
	e Connects the different activities that connect to each other	2.12, 2.13	
B1 Technologies that affect business and finance	a The key features of the fourth industrial revolution	3.2, 3.5, 3.7	
	b The key technologies that define and drive the digital world	3.1, 3.3, 3.4, 3.6, 3.8, 3.9, 3.10, 3.11, 3.12, 3.13, 3.14, 3.15	
B2 How the finance function uses digital technologies to fulfil its roles	a Digital technology	4.2, 4.14	
	b Digital mindsets	4.9	
	c Automation and the future of work	4.1, 4.3, 4.4, 4.5, 4.6, 4.7, 4.8, 4.10, 4.12, 4.16, 4.17, 4.18, 4.19, 4.20	
	d Ethics of technology usage	4.11, 4.13, 4.15, 4.21, 4.22	
C1 Data and the finance function	a General usage of data in finance	5.1, 5.4, 5.8, 5.10	
	b Specific usage of data in primary activities of finance	5.2, 5.3, 5.5, 5.6, 5.7, 5.9, 5.11, 5.12, 5.13, 5.14, 5.15	

Lead outcome	Component outcome	Questions	Completed
C2 Data to create and preserve value for organisations	a Data strategy and planning	6.1, 6.2, 6.5, 6.9	
	b Data engineering, extraction and mining	6.3, 6.4, 6.6, 6.7, 6.10	
	c Data modelling, manipulation and analysis	6.11, 6.12, 6.13, 6.14	
	d Data and insight communication	6.8, 6.15	
D1 The structure and shape of the finance function	a Evolution of the shape of the finance function	7.1, 7.2, 7.3, 7.5, 7.11, 7.12, 7.13	
	b Shape of the finance function in the digital era	7.4, 7.6, 7.7, 7.8, 7.9, 7.10, 7.14, 7.15, 7.16, 7.17	
D2 What each level of the finance function does	a Finance operations	8.1, 8.2, 8.3, 8.4, 8.5, 8.6, 8.7	
	b Specialist areas including financial reporting and financial planning and analysis (FP&A)	8.8, 8.9, 8.10, 8.11	
	c Strategic partnering for value	8.12, 8.13	
	d Strategic leadership of the finance team	8.14, 8.15	
E1 The finance function's relationship to operations	a Main role of operations	9.2, 9.3, 9.5, 9.7, 9.8, 9.10, 9.13, 9.23	
	b Areas of interface with finance	9.1, 9.4, 9.6, 9.9, 9.11, 9.12, 9.14, 9.16, 9.17, 9.18, 9.19, 9.20, 9.21, 9.22	
	c Key performance indicators	9.15	
E2 The finance function's relationship to sales and marketing	a Main role of sales and marketing	10.1, 10.2, 10.3, 10.6, 10.7, 10.8, 10.10, 10.11, 10.13, 10.14, 10.15, 10.16, 10.18, 10.20, 10.21	
	b Areas of interface with finance	10.4, 10.5, 10.9, 10.12, 10.19, 10.22	
	c Key performance indicators	10.17	

Lead outcome	Component outcome	Questions	Completed
E3 The finance function's relationship to human resources	a Main role of human resources	11.1, 11.2, 11.3, 11.4, 11.5, 11.6, 11.7, 11.8, 11.9, 11.10, 11.11, 11.12, 11.13, 11.14, 11.15, 11.17, 11.18, 11.19, 11.20, 11.21	
	b-c Areas of interface with finance and key performance indicators	11.16	
E4 The finance function's relationship to IT	a Main role of IT	12.1, 12.2, 12.3, 12.4, 12.5, 12.6, 12.7, 12.8, 12.10, 12.11, 12.12, 12.13, 12.14, 12.15, 12.16, 12.17, 12.18	
	b-c Areas of interface with finance and key performance indicators	12.9	

Examination structure

The Objective Test exam

Pass mark	70%
Format	Computer-based assessment
Duration	90 minutes
Number of questions	60
Marking	No partial marking – each question marked correct or incorrect All questions carry the same weighting (ie same marks)
Weighting	As per syllabus areas All representative task statements from the examination blueprint will be covered
Question Types	Multiple choice Multiple response Drag and drop Gap fill Hot spot
Booking availability	On demand
Results	Immediate

What the examiner means

The table below has been prepared by CIMA to further help you interpret the syllabus and learning outcomes and the meaning of questions.

You will see that there are five skills levels you may be expected to demonstrate, ranging from Remembering and Understanding to Evaluation. CIMA Certificate subjects only use levels 1 to 3, but in CIMA's Professional qualification the entire hierarchy will be used.

	Skills level	Verbs used	Definition
Level 5	**Evaluation** *The examination or assessment of problems, and use of judgment to draw conclusions*	Advise	Counsel, inform or notify
		Assess	Evaluate or estimate the nature, ability or quality of
		Evaluate	Appraise or assess the value of
		Recommend	Propose a course of action
		Review	Assess and evaluate in order, to change if necessary
		Select	Choose an option or course of action after consideration of the alternatives

Skills level		Verbs used	Definition
Level 4	**Analysis** *The examination and study of the interrelationships of separate areas in order to identify causes and find evidence to support inferences*	Align	Arrange in an orderly way
		Analyse	Examine in detail the structure of
		Communicate	Share or exchange information
		Compare and contrast	Show the similarities and/or differences between
		Develop	Grow and expand a concept
		Discuss	Examine in detail by argument
		Examine	Inspect thoroughly
		Monitor	Observe and check the progress of
		Prioritise	Place in order of priority or sequence for action
		Produce	Create or bring into existence
Level 3	**Application** *The use or demonstration of knowledge, concepts or techniques*	Apply	Put to practical use
		Calculate	Ascertain or reckon mathematically
		Conduct	Organise and carry out
		Demonstrate	Prove with certainty or exhibit by practical means
		Determine	Ascertain or establish exactly by research or calculation
		Perform	Carry out, accomplish, or fulfil
		Prepare	Make or get ready for use
		Reconcile	Make or prove consistent/compatible
		Record	Keep a permanent account of facts, events or transactions
		Use	Apply a technique or concept

	Skills level	Verbs used	Definition
Level 1/2	**Remembering and understanding** *The perception and comprehension of the significance of an area utilising knowledge gained*	Define	Give the exact meaning of
		Describe	Communicate the key features of
		Distinguish	Highlight the differences between
		Explain	Make clear or intelligible/state the meaning or purpose of
		Identify	Recognise, establish or select after consideration
		Illustrate	Use an example to describe or explain something
		List	Make a list of
		Recognise	Identify/recall
		State	Express, fully or clearly, the details/facts of
		Outline	Give a summary of
		Understand	Comprehend ideas, concepts and techniques

(CIMA exam blueprint, 2023/2024)

How to pass

Good exam technique

The best approach to the computer-based assessment (CBA)

You're not likely to have a great deal of spare time during the CBA itself, so you must make sure you don't waste a single minute.

You should:

1.   Click 'Next' for any that have long scenarios or are very complex and return to these later

2.   When you reach the 60th question, use the Review Screen to return to any questions you skipped past or any you flagged for review

Here's how the tools in the exam will help you to do this in a controlled and efficient way.

The 'Next' button

What does it do? This will move you on to the next question whether or not you have completed the one you are on.

When should I use it? Use this to move through the exam on your first pass through if you encounter a question that you suspect is going to take you a long time to answer. The Review Screen (see below) will help you to return to these questions later in the exam.

The 'Flag for Review' button

What does it do? This button will turn the icon yellow and when you reach the end of the exam questions you will be told that you have flagged specific questions for review. If the exam time runs out before you have reviewed any flagged questions, they will be submitted as they are.

When should I use it? Use this when you've answered a question but you're not completely comfortable with your answer. If there is time left at the end, you can quickly come back via the Review Screen (see below), but if time runs out at least it will submit your current answer. Do not use the Flag for Review button too often or you will end up with too long a list to review at the end. Important note – studies have shown that you are usually best to stick with your first instincts!

The Review Screen

What does it do? This screen appears after you click 'Next' on the 60th question. It shows you any incomplete questions and any you have flagged for review. It allows you to jump back to specific questions or work through all your incomplete questions or work through all your flagged for review questions.

When should I use it? As soon as you've completed your first run through the exam and reached the 60th question. The very first thing to do is to work through all your incomplete questions as they will all be marked as incorrect if you don't submit an answer for these in the remaining time. Importantly, this will also help to pick up any questions you thought you'd completed but didn't answer properly (eg you only picked two answer options in a multi-response question that required three answers to be selected). After you've submitted answers for all your incomplete questions you should use the Review Screen to work through all the questions you flagged for review.

The different Objective Test question types

Passing your CBA is all about demonstrating your understanding of the technical syllabus content. You will find this easier to do if you are comfortable with the different types of Objective Test questions that you will encounter in the CBA, especially if you have a practised approach to each one.

You will find yourself continuously practising these styles of questions throughout your Objective Test programme. This way you will check and reinforce your technical knowledge at the same time as becoming more and more comfortable with your approach to each style of question.

Multiple choice

Standard multiple choice items provide four options. One option is correct and the other three are incorrect. Incorrect options will be plausible, so you should expect to have to use detailed, syllabus-specific knowledge to identify the correct answer rather than relying on common sense.

Multiple response

A multiple response item is the same as a multiple choice question, except more than one response is required. You will normally (but not always) be told how many options you need to select.

Drag and drop

Drag and drop questions require you to drag a 'token' onto a pre-defined area. These tokens can be images or text. This type of question is effective at testing the order of events, labelling a diagram or linking events to outcomes.

Gap fill

Gap fill (or 'fill in the blank') questions require you to type a short numerical response. You should carefully follow the instructions in the question in terms of how to type your answer – eg the correct number of decimal places.

Hot spot

These questions require you to identify an area or location on an image by clicking on it. This is commonly used to identify a specific point on a graph or diagram.

A final word on time management

Time does funny things in an exam!

Scientific studies have shown that humans have great difficulty in judging how much time has passed if they are concentrating fully on a challenging task (which your CBA should be!).

You can try this for yourself. Have a go at, say, five questions for your paper, and notice what time you start at. As soon as you finish the last question try to estimate how long it took you and then compare to your watch. The majority of us tend to underestimate how quickly time passes and this can cost you dearly in a full exam if you don't take steps to keep track of time.

So, the key thing here is to set yourself sensible milestones, and then get into the habit of regularly checking how you are doing against them:

- You need to develop an internal warning system – 'I've now spent more than three minutes on this one calculation – this is too long and I need to move on!' (less for a narrative question!)

- Keep your milestones in mind (eg approximately 30 questions done after 45 mins). If you are a distance from where you should be then adjust your pace accordingly. This usually means speeding up but can mean slowing down a bit if needs be, as you may be rushing when you don't need to and increasing the risk of making silly mistakes.

A full exam will be a mix of questions you find harder and those you find easier, and in the real CBA the order is randomised, so you could get a string of difficult questions right at the beginning of your exam. Do not be put off by this – they should be balanced later by a series of questions you find easier.

Objective test questions

1 Role of the finance function

1.1 Corporate governance is best described as:

- ○ A code for organisational direction, administration and control
- ○ Stakeholder guidelines
- ○ A system of penalties for unethical behaviour
- ○ The relationship between an organisation and the government

1.2 Which of the following is the objective of effective business processes?

- ○ Creating the maximum output
- ○ Creating value for money products
- ○ Creating the maximum output for minimum input
- ○ Creating the best quality output from the available inputs

1.3 In order to establish whether a particular organisation should be classified as a business or not, it would be necessary to enquire as to the nature of its:

- ○ Primary objective
- ○ Mission
- ○ Vision
- ○ Secondary objective

1.4 Which of the following characteristics is NOT normally associated with a Non-Governmental Organisation (NGO)?

- ○ Furthering humanitarian causes
- ○ Championing social causes
- ○ Making profits
- ○ Exercising independence

1.5 Which of the following is the primary financial objective of public sector organisations?

- ○ Profitability
- ○ Efficient use of resources
- ○ Avoidance of loss
- ○ Maximisation of charitable donations

BPP
LEARNING
MEDIA

1.6 According to Carroll and Buchholtz a company that was trying to avoid tax, by employing legal loopholes, could defend its actions by claiming it was engaged in which layer of corporate social responsibility?

○ Economic

○ Legal

○ Ethical

○ Philanthropic

1.7 Which of the following is a not for profit organisation?

○ Sole traders

○ Partnerships

○ Mutual organisations

○ Public limited companies

1.8 A company may seek to improve corporate governance by ensuring that:

○ The chairman and chief executive are the same individual in order to avoid confusion over who has responsibility for running the company

○ The chairman and chief executive are different individuals in order to prevent one person having too much power within the company

○ The chairman and chief executive are different individuals in case one dies or becomes incapacitated due to ill health

○ The company chairman does not take up outside directorships

1.9 Which of the following would be identified as a problem with the role of non-executive director?

○ External stakeholder security

○ Time available to devote to the role

○ Objective viewpoint

○ Dual nature of the role, firstly as full board members and secondly, as a strong, independent element

1.10 Which of the following are consequences of technological connectedness?
Select all that apply

☐ Reduced levels of competition

☐ Faster and easier communication

☐ Changes to who competitors and stakeholders are

☐ Increased power of stakeholders

☐ Rules of business becoming less dynamic

1.11   **Which of the following statements concerning a written code of ethics is correct?**

    ○   It sets out the company's attitude to risk

    ○   It should be independent of management actions

    ○   It supports non-compliance

    ○   It is based on the law

1.12   **With regard to Porter's five forces analysis and new entrants into a market, which of the following pairs of statements is correct?**

○	Encourages new entrants High competition	Erects a barrier to new entrants Low capital costs
○	Encourages new entrants A monopoly supplier of a vital component	Erects a barrier to new entrants High competition
○	Encourages new entrants A monopoly supplier of a vital component	Erects a barrier to new entrants One large customer
○	Encourages new entrants Low competition	Erects a barrier to new entrants High capital costs

1.13   ABC Co sells mobile telephones. Each phone sold is supplied with a charger, earpiece, car charger and other accessories which can only be used with ABC Co phones. Its predictive text style is also very different to that of other manufacturers.

    To which of Porter's five forces is this strategy intended to respond?

    ○   Bargaining power of suppliers

    ○   Bargaining power of customers

    ○   Threat of new entrants

    ○   Intensity of competitive rivalry

1.14   **Which of the following has become an established best practice in corporate governance?**

    ○   An increasingly prominent role for non-executive directors

    ○   An increase in the powers of external auditors

    ○   Greater accountability for directors who are in breach of their fiduciary duties

    ○   A requirement for all companies to establish an internal audit function

1.15   The finance function value matrix analyses what finance functions do and why they
        perform those activities in terms of creating and preserving value.

        **Which area of the matrix concerns the finance function acting as a trusted source of
        management information?**

        ○   Data integrity

        ○   Value analysis

        ○   Stewardship

        ○   Value enabling

1.16   **Which of the following measures will help an organisation to limit its environmental
        impact?**

        I   Recycling waste
        II   Using energy efficient electrical appliances
        III   Selecting suppliers carefully
        IV   Buying raw materials locally

        ○   I and II only

        ○   II and IV only

        ○   I and III only

        ○   I, II, III and IV

1.17   Darlene, a part CIMA qualified analyst, has been asked to replace her manager, who has a
        tickly cough and feels poorly. Initially Darlene is excited because her manager deals
        directly with the client, making this a prestigious job and giving her a chance to shine. She
        has realised, however, that her manager is required to run the job because she is fully CIMA
        qualified. The CEO of the company has told Darlene that she worries too much, and should
        seize this opportunity with both hands.

        **Which TWO CIMA ethical guidelines would Darlene be breaking if she went along with the
        plan?**

        ☐   Integrity

        ☐   Objectivity

        ☐   Professional competence and due care

        ☐   Confidentiality

        ☐   Professional behaviour

1.18   **Which of the following describes the basis of CIMA's Code of Ethics for professional
        accountants?**

        ○   A framework of fundamental principles

        ○   A policy document containing strict rules

        ○   A policy of penalties for non-compliance with general guidelines

        ○   A range of principles for best practice

1.19   Taking an organisation's strategic goals and critical success factors and turning them into
        a detailed roadmap from where the organisation is to where it wants to be.

        Which key activity of the finance function does this describe?

        ○   Financial reporting

        ○   Performance management

        ○   Planning and forecasting

        ○   Resource allocation

1.20   **What is the usual purpose of codes of practice on corporate governance?**

        ○   To establish legally binding requirements to which all companies must adhere

        ○   To set down detailed rules to regulate the ways in which companies must operate

        ○   To provide guidance on the standards of best practice that companies should adopt

        ○   To provide a comprehensive framework for management and administration

2   Activities of finance professionals

2.1   Justin Co has a major stakeholder who in the past has been able to exert considerable
        influence over the environmental impact of the company's manufacturing operations.
        Specifically, as a result of one recent campaign orchestrated by this stakeholder, a
        production facility was temporarily closed down for three weeks. The stakeholder writes
        regularly to the company's chairman regarding a range of environmental issues
        surrounding the company.

        **In terms of Mendelow's Matrix the company would be advised to pursue which of the
        following strategies in respect of this stakeholder?**

        ○   Keep this stakeholder informed at all times about the company

        ○   Keep this stakeholder satisfied with regard to the company and its strategies

        ○   Use minimum effort with regard to this stakeholder because he always complains

        ○   Treat this stakeholder as a key player when formulating future strategies

2.2   Successful business partnering requires accountants to develop skillsets in certain areas.

        **Which THREE of the following are skills associated with the ability to integrate, apply and
        communicate skillset?**

        ☐   Accounting skills

        ☐   Analytical skills

        ☐   Commercial curiosity

        ☐   Passion for business

        ☐   Preparedness to challenge

        ☐   Business understanding

2.3 **Which type of data consists of standard metrics which are well tracked and understood by an organisation?**

○ Financial data

○ Enterprise data

○ Big data

○ Informal data

2.4 **Gathering external data from a range of sources is known as:**

○ Market research

○ Environmental scanning

○ Formal data collection

○ Research and development

2.5 **Which TWO of the following are examples of conflict between an organisation's stakeholders caused by differences in their aims and objectives?**

☐ Business operations may be prevented by managerial short-termism

☐ Owners of small businesses may lose control of the organisation when it grows and it becomes necessary to appoint managers to run the business

☐ Mass marketing campaigns may require an increase in the quality of products produced

☐ The financial independence of an organisation may be reduced when additional shares or loans are required

☐ Staffing levels are increased as a consequence of increased capital investment

2.6 Two of Sunshine Tours Co's stakeholder groups are putting the company under pressure to improve its return on investment.

These are most likely to comprise which TWO of the following groups?

☐ Shareholders

☐ Customers

☐ Bankers

☐ Suppliers

☐ Employees

2.7 **Identifying inaccuracies in data and modifying or deleting them is known as:**

○ Data analysis

○ Data cleansing

○ Data connection

○ Data storage

2.8 **Which of the following statements about insights is correct?**

○ Insights are basic financial information

○ Insights are records of what has happened in the past

○ Insights are indications of the drivers of value for an organisation

○ Insights are irrelevant to decision making

2.9 **Which level of data analysis asks the question 'Why did it happen?'**

○ Reporting

○ Prediction

○ Monitoring

○ Analysis

2.10 **Which of the following is an example of an internal stakeholder?**

○ A shareholder

○ An non-executive director

○ A manager

○ A supplier

2.11 Effective communication is based on several factors.

Which communication factor considers how and where the communication is received?

○ Audience

○ Frequency

○ Format

○ Stakeholder management

2.12 Finance functions often embed themselves and work alongside different business areas, rather than just being a separate business function.

What concept is described above?

○ Strategic partnering for value

○ Business partnering

○ Segregation

○ Outsourcing

BPP
LEARNING
MEDIA

2.13   **Which TWO of the following are ways that the finance function connects the different activities in an organisation?**

☐   Appraisal systems

☐   Budgeting

☐   Process design

☐   Target marketing

☐   Information systems

2.14   Successful business partnering requires accountants to develop skillsets in certain areas.

Which of the following are skills associated with effective business partnering relationships?

Select all that apply

☐   Empathy with business

☐   Analytical skills

☐   Commercial curiosity

☐   Compelling communication

☐   Preparedness to challenge

☐   Professional objectivity

2.15   **Which of the following statements concerning the cost of information is correct?**

○   Information should have a value greater than the cost of obtaining it

○   Information should have a value less than the cost of obtaining it

○   Value cannot be placed on information and therefore it does not matter how much it costs to obtain it

○   The cost of information does not include the time users spend working out what it means

3   Technologies used in business and finance

3.1   Aggra Co has a supercomputer on site. This computer is capable of a great deal of work. Aggra Co has connected the computer to the internet. It has started charging companies who wish to do scientific analysis for use of the supercomputer by the minute. Companies find this agreeable because their typical usage doesn't justify owning a supercomputer. They put complex inputs into the supercomputer, which comes up with an easy to understand output.

This arrangement is described as:

○   Cloud service

○   WAN

○   Expert system

○   Grid computing

3.2 Which type of technology is powering the fourth industrial revolution?

○ Electronic technology

○ Microchip technology

○ Digital technology

○ Information technology

3.3 Which of the following statements concerning big data analytics is correct?

○ Big data analytics relies on digital information

○ Big data analytics relies on written information

○ Big data analytics relies on verbal information

○ Big data analytics relies on confidential information

3.4 Which of the following statements concerning big data analytics is NOT correct?

○ Big data analytics enables large quantities of data to examined quickly

○ Big data analytics improves organisational decision making

○ Big data analytics enables cost reduction

○ Big data analytics shifts organisational focus from individual customers to groups of customers

3.5 There are several features of the fourth industrial revolution that distinguish it from previous industrial revolutions. One example is that this revolution is disrupting industries in almost every country, rather than just a few specific countries.

Which feature does this describe?

○ Velocity

○ Effect

○ Scope

○ Application

3.6 Which of the following is a key feature of big data?

○ Accessibility

○ Volume

○ Complicated

○ Redundancy

3.7   **Which of the following are changes or dynamics of the fourth industrial revolution? Select all that apply**

☐   Increased transportation and communication costs

☐   Fewer opportunities to enhance existing products

☐   Jobs being replaced by automation

☐   Greater customer expectations for products and services provided

☐   Reduced scope for collaboration and innovation between businesses

3.8   **The ability of systems to perform routine activities without the input of a human is known as:**

○   Artificial intelligence

○   Data analytics

○   Process automation

○   Data visualisation

3.9   **The ability of a computer system to assist a human operator to make decisions and solve problems is known as:**

○   Internet of things

○   Process automation

○   Distributed ledger technology

○   Artificial intelligence

3.10   **Which method of data visualisation is often used to present variance analysis and is designed so that the eye focuses on the most significant movements first?**

○   Waterfall charts

○   Dashboards

○   Line charts

○   Mapping charts

3.11   **Which method of data visualisation provides a summary of four or five relevant drivers that give an overview of a business area?**

○   Tables

○   Line charts

○   Dashboards

○   Waterfall charts

3.12   **Which feature of blockchain refers to the fact that there are many copies of a blockchain ledger, but no master copy?**

    ○   Programmability

    ○   Prevalence

    ○   Propagation

    ○   Permanence

3.13   **Which of the following statements concerning blockchain is correct?**

    ○   There is a master version of the blockchain that propagates out through all existing copies

    ○   New transactions cannot be added to the blockchain

    ○   Blockchains cannot be used to create so-called 'smart-contracts'

    ○   Past transactions on a blockchain can only be edited with the consent of the majority of other holders of the same blockchain

3.14   **Short message service (SMS) and multimedia messaging service (MMS) are examples of early uses of which of the following technologies?**

    ○   Internet of things

    ○   Blockchain

    ○   Mobile technology

    ○   Process automation

3.15   **Devices that can transfer data over the internet without requiring human-to-human or human-to-computer interaction are known as:**

    ○   Distributed ledger technology

    ○   Mobile technology

    ○   Internet of things

    ○   Artificial intelligence

4   Digital technologies and the finance function

4.1   Hayley Porter is an accountant with Worricker Co. Hayley was recently asked to join a project team analysing data to provide information that will be used as the basis of a management decision.

    It appears, therefore, that she has been recruited into this project team in order to exploit her expertise in:

    ○   Financial reporting

    ○   Treasury

    ○   Internal audit

    ○   Management accounting

4.2   **Which of the following is a use of distributed ledgers by the finance function?**

      ○   Analysing movements in the currency markets

      ○   As a form of cloud accounting

      ○   Verifying the ownership of assets

      ○   As a method of communicating insights

4.3   The central bank has announced a 2% increase in interest rates.

      This decision has the most direct impact on which component of the finance function?

      ○   Management accounting

      ○   Treasury

      ○   Financial reporting

      ○   Internal audit

4.4   **Which component of the finance function has responsibility for ensuring that the organisation's rules and policies are complied with?**

      ○   Internal audit

      ○   Management accounting

      ○   Treasury

      ○   Financial reporting

4.5   **Which of the following processes in the financial reporting part of the finance function has the potential to be automated?**

      ○   Calculation of variances

      ○   Investment appraisal calculations

      ○   Creation of statutory accounts

      ○   Monitoring of transactions for suspicious activity

4.6   **Which of the following processes in the internal audit function have the potential to be automated?**
      Select all that apply

      ☐   Simulations of cyberattacks to test IT controls

      ☐   Automatic cashflow forecasting

      ☐   Vulnerability testing to identify weaknesses in the business

      ☐   Automatic downloading of bank transactions

      ☐   Assisted budgeting based on current actual figures

4.7 **In a typical finance function, preparation of budgets and budgetary control would usually be the responsibility of which of the following roles?**

○ A financial reporting accountant

○ A management accountant

○ The treasurer

○ The finance director

4.8 Harold is an accountant with Farnworth Co. He was recently asked to join a project team looking into the company's compliance with both FRC and IASB standards.

It appears, therefore, that Harold has been recruited into this project team in order to exploit his expertise in:

○ Financial reporting

○ Performance measurement

○ Capital budgeting

○ Strategic management accounting

4.9 **Which TWO of the following are key aspects of a digital mindset?**

☐ Learning knowledge for life

☐ Dealing with complexity

☐ Letting others take responsibility for your digital literacy

☐ Working in a creative and agile way

☐ Being sceptical of change in the digital environment

4.10 **Which THREE of the following are functions associated with treasury management?**

☐ Arranging finance

☐ 'What if' scenario planning for investment appraisal

☐ Analysis of financial accounting ratios

☐ Revaluation of company assets

☐ Analysis of operating variances

☐ Management of foreign currency holdings

4.11 **Which of the following is a correct statement concerning the principles of data protection legislation in the UK?**

○ Data may be held for any purpose

○ Individuals must be notified of the purpose of holding the data within a month of it being collected

○ Data held must be adequate, relevant and not excessive

○ Organisations may correct data found to be inaccurate or misleading if they consider it necessary

BPP
LEARNING
MEDIA

4.12 In terms of automation and the finance function, a human-only activity should be used where:

- ○ There is routine processing of transactions
- ○ Technology can augment human intelligence
- ○ There is application of knowledge across a range of different tasks
- ○ Errors might arise that need resolving

4.13 Which of the following aspects of information technology does NOT raise ethical issues?

- ○ The power of computers doubles every 18 months
- ○ The cost of storing data is declining
- ○ The increasing use of fraud detection systems in e-commerce
- ○ Increasing ease of transferring data between separate networks

4.14 Which TWO of the following technologies might be used where an organisation's finance manager views insights created by their team on a tablet whilst working away from the office?

- ☐ Data visualisation
- ☐ 3-D printing
- ☐ Process automation
- ☐ Blockchain
- ☐ Mobile technology

4.15 Which of the following is NOT a right granted to individuals by data protection legislation in the UK?

- ○ Access
- ○ Erasure
- ○ Rectification
- ○ Evaluation

4.16 Which THREE of the following correctly describe the advantages of organisations using budgets?

- ☐ Capacity
- ☐ Responsibility
- ☐ Understanding
- ☐ Motivation
- ☐ Performance
- ☐ Telling

4.17   Brian is the treasury accountant for Chuck Ltd. Brian is concerned that the company's
       working capital situation is poor, and is considering implementing more aggressive working
       capital management policies.

       **Which of the following is a potential consequence of a more aggressive working
       capital policy?**

       ○   Increased inventory obsolescence

       ○   Increased material costs

       ○   Increased sales from longer credit periods

       ○   Increased bad and doubtful debts

4.18   **Which of the following correctly describes the scope of Internal Audit departments?**

       ○   Acting independently

       ○   Given an opinion on the truth and fairness of the financial statements

       ○   Reporting the effectiveness of risk management procedures

       ○   Reviewing the effectiveness of the audit committee

4.19   **Which TWO of the following describe the symptoms of fraud?**

       ☐   Staff morale being low

       ☐   Staff not taking holiday

       ☐   Domination by powerful staff members

       ☐   Complex corporate structures

       ☐   Lavish lifestyles of staff, not in keeping with their salary

4.20   Molly has worked in the Internal Audit department of Theta plc, a company listed on a
       major stock exchange for three years. Molly has just heard that her father has been
       appointed as a non-executive director of the company, and plans to join the audit
       committee.

       **Which of the following limitations of Internal Audit arises from the situation
       described above?**

       ○   Threat to independence

       ○   Organisational constraints

       ○   Poorly qualified or experienced staff

       ○   Self-interest threat

4.21   **Which of the following activities is illegal?**

       ○   Tax avoidance

       ○   Tax mitigation

       ○   Tax evasion

       ○   Tax minimisation

4.22 Reducing tax liability through conduct that does not frustrate the intentions of Parliament when the law was created is known as?

- ○ Tax evasion
- ○ Tax limitation
- ○ Tax avoidance
- ○ Tax mitigation

5 Data and the finance function

5.1 Improved consistency of data due to holding and maintaining a single data source shared by multiple users.

Which novel technology does the statement describe an advantage of?

- ○ Internet of things
- ○ Blockchain
- ○ Cloud computing
- ○ Data visualisation

5.2 Understanding customer preferences to identify features of a product or service that adds value for them.

This is an example of how data and information can be used to improve an organisation's:

- ○ Operational efficiency
- ○ Sales and marketing
- ○ Digital assets
- ○ Financial performance

5.3 **What is the strategic objective of collecting data about customers and improving the organisation's understanding of their needs?**

- ○ To create value
- ○ To minimise product returns
- ○ To maximise product quality
- ○ To improve online reviews

5.4 Improved communication of information that is more effective and rich.

Which novel technology does the statement describe an advantage of?

- ○ Data visualisation
- ○ Data analytics
- ○ Mobile technology
- ○ Artificial intelligence

5.5 Allows fast assembly of prototype products. Changes can be made quickly and sent to any business location.

Which novel technology does the statement describe an advantage of?

○ Artificial intelligence

○ Process automation

○ 3-D printing

○ Data analytics

5.6 **Which of the following are sources of customer data?**
Select all that apply

☐ Responses from online promotions, advertising and emails

☐ Electronic data interchange systems

☐ Enterprise resource planning systems

☐ Tablet and phone apps

☐ Reverse logistics systems

5.7 **Reverse logistics systems are used in which function of an organisation?**

○ Finance

○ Sales and marketing

○ Operations

○ HR

5.8 Allows decision makers to access information wherever they are, provided they have access to a phone signal.

Which novel technology does the statement describe an advantage of?

○ Data analytics

○ Big data

○ Mobile technology

○ Blockchain

5.9 **Which THREE of the following are sources of operational data?**

☐ Inventory management systems

☐ Relationship management software

☐ Visitor data from the organisation's website

☐ Quality control systems

☐ Manufacturing resource planning systems

☐ Online market trends

BPP
LEARNING
MEDIA

5.10 Allows patterns or trends to be found in data or information where they would previously have been impossible or too time-consuming to identify.

Which novel technology does the statement describe an advantage of?

- ○ Big data
- ○ Data analytics
- ○ Process automation
- ○ Data visualisation

5.11 **Which type of operational inefficiency can be identified by analysing quality control systems?**

- ○ Slow moving product lines
- ○ High levels of rework
- ○ Delays in transferring documents between the organisation and third parties
- ○ Poor working capital management

5.12 **Which of the following statements concerning digital assets is correct?**

- ○ Digital assets' ownership rights usually require specific protection
- ○ Digital assets are not permanent assets
- ○ Digital assets are not capable of being copied
- ○ Digital assets are a form of tangible asset

5.13 There are a number of considerations associated with increased data use by organisations.

Which of the following is an impact of increased data use on data dependence?

- ○ The organisation is vulnerable to errors and poor quality data
- ○ Investment is required in cloud storage
- ○ The most effective data mining tools are required
- ○ Appropriate methods of distributing the data are required

5.14 **Which THREE of the following are rights granted to individuals under the Data Protection Act 2018?**

- ☐ To be informed
- ☐ Compensation
- ☐ Access
- ☐ Restrict processing
- ☐ Reversal
- ☐ Explanation

5.15 Which of the following is a principle of corporate digital responsibility that is affected by increased data use?

○ Transparency

○ Competence

○ Erasure

○ Value creation

6 Using data to create and preserve value

6.1 A measuring or recording device.

Which element of a feedback system does this describe?

○ Sensor

○ Comparator

○ Effector

○ Higher-level controller

6.2 **Which of the following options will NOT help an organisation to close an information gap within the operations system?**

○ Reconfiguration of existing systems

○ Purchase of a new system

○ Development of new parts for existing systems

○ Purchase of information regarding the business environment

6.3 **Which of the following are found at the very top of a business intelligence stack? Select all that apply**

☐ Real time access

☐ IT infrastructure

☐ Data warehouse

☐ Dashboards

☐ Systems

6.4 **In terms of a data ETL system, what does the 'E' refer to?**

○ Erasure

○ Extraction

○ Exploratory

○ Effect

6.5 An actual result is analysed in relation to a plan or standard.

Which element of a feedback system performs this role?

○ Effector

○ Higher-level controller

○ Comparator

○ Sensor

6.6 **What happens during the 'load' phase of a data ETL system?**

○ Source data is read from the existing system

○ Source data is uploaded into the transformation software

○ Transformed data is written into a target database

○ Transformed data is transmitted to data visualisation software

6.7 **In terms of a business intelligence stack, what system allows managers without specialist IT or analytical expertise to drill into and view data in different ways to identify hidden relationships?**

○ ETL systems

○ Data warehouse

○ Online analytical processing, data mining, query and reporting systems

○ CRM systems

6.8 **Which elements of a business intelligence stack provide storage capacity for big data?**

○ Warehouse management

○ IT infrastructure

○ Dashboards

○ ETL systems

6.9 Rohan works as a supervisor in the operations function of an organisation. Last month he received a number of negative variances from a member of the management accounting team and put in place controls to prevent them happening again.

In terms of a feedback system, Rohan works as:

○ A higher-level controller

○ A comparator

○ A sensor

○ An effector

6.10 **Which of the following is found at the very bottom of an organisation's business intelligence stack?**

- ○ Web
- ○ ETL systems
- ○ IT infrastructure
- ○ Legacy systems

6.11 **Which of the following is NOT a stage of data modelling?**

- ○ Conceptual model
- ○ Logical model
- ○ Speculative model
- ○ Physical model

6.12 **Which of the following describes data manipulation?**

- ○ Analysis of the information needs required to support business processes
- ○ Processing data to support decision making
- ○ Reorganising or transforming data to make it easier to read or more meaningful
- ○ Communicating data to decision makers

6.13 **Which type of data analysis involves finding new relationships or features in a data set?**

- ○ Confirmatory data analysis
- ○ Predictive data analysis
- ○ Exploratory data analysis
- ○ Text data analysis

6.14 **Which type of data analysis involves proving or disproving an hypothesis?**

- ○ Text data analysis
- ○ Exploratory data analysis
- ○ Confirmatory data analysis
- ○ Predictive data analysis

6.15 The finance function has a key role to play in data cleansing.

Which characteristic of big data is this role of finance related to?

- ○ Volume
- ○ Velocity
- ○ Veracity
- ○ Variety

7 Structure and shape of the finance function

7.1 Romulus Co and Remus Co have recently agreed to co-operate to exploit the possibilities that both companies have in a particular overseas market. No separate company has been established for this purpose as the companies' chief executives, who have known each other for many years, have agreed matters informally.

This arrangement is an example of a:

○ Licensing agreement

○ Joint venture

○ Strategic alliance

○ Outsourcing agreement

7.2 **Which of the following are features of the contemporary finance function?**
Select all that apply

☐ Generating financial statements

☐ Creating and communicating insights

☐ Processing routine transactions

☐ Performing variance calculations

☐ Analysing information that has often been generated automatically

7.3 **Which of the following organisational structures encourages employee flexibility and multiple reporting?**

○ Matrix

○ Centralised

○ Functional

○ Divisional

7.4 **Which of the following is the cause of the segregated structure of the finance function?**

○ Offshoring

○ Outsourcing

○ Shared service centres

○ Business partnering

7.5 **Mintzberg's design of an effective organisation does NOT include which of the following categories?**

○ Technostructure

○ Outsource partners

○ Operating core

○ Strategic apex

7.6 **Which of the following is NOT an advantage of having a shared finance service centre?**

○ Tailored response

○ Economies of scale

○ Reduction in cost

○ Better quality service

7.7 **Which of the following is the cause of the contemporary diamond shape of the finance function?**

○ Process automation

○ Big data

○ Data visualisation

○ Mobile technology

7.8 M Co has decided to outsource its IT support to N Co.

Which of the following are DISADVANTAGES to M Co as a result of this decision?

I   M Co becomes a more complex organisation
II Urgent IT issues at M Co may not be resolved as quickly
III Ongoing IT costs of M Co will increase
IV Long term contracts with N Co are prone to disruption

○ I and III

○ II and III

○ I and IV

○ II and IV

7.9 **A client-vendor relationship is a feature of which of the following?**

○ An outsourced IT function

○ Enterprise-wide systems

○ Social networking

○ Virtual team working

7.10 **Service Level Agreements are normally associated with:**

○ Job reductions negotiated with staff groups

○ Deskilling

○ Agreed appraisal outcomes

○ Outsourcing

7.11 **Which of the following is a benefit of a functional organisational structure?**

○   A culture of innovation is encouraged.

○   The organisation can achieve economies of scale.

○   Problems of hierarchy are prevented.

○   Horizontal co-ordination is facilitated.

7.12 **Which of the following is NOT a benefit of a strategic alliance?**

○   Strict contractual control over the business partner

○   Increased barriers to entry

○   More selling power

○   More buying power

7.13 **The term 'scalar chain' refers to what within an organisation?**

○   Elements of the organisation's product portfolio

○   A range of employee incentives to improve motivation

○   Line of command

○   Span of control

7.14 **Transferring some part of an organisation's activities to a subsidiary in another country is an example of:**

○   Free trade

○   Outsourcing

○   Offshoring

○   Delegation

7.15 **Which of the following statements about outsourcing is true?**

○   In order to maintain control, the organisation should outsource activities in areas of its own core competence.

○   Outsourcing to external contractors harnesses specialist expertise, but at the cost of lost economies of scale.

○   Outsourcing carries commercial and reputational risks.

○   Outsourcing saves all the costs associated with performing a task in-house.

7.16   B plc is considering whether to make or buy a vital component. If B plc wishes to manufacture the component themselves, they will need to build a specialist lathe to machine the part to the specification required.

Which of the following is most relevant to this 'make or buy' decision?

- ○   Physical asset specificity
- ○   Human asset specificity
- ○   Temporal specificity
- ○   Site specificity

7.17   **In Transaction Cost Theory which of the following is NOT an aspect of the 'make or buy decision' per Williamson?**

- ○   Uncertainty
- ○   Frequency
- ○   Standardisation
- ○   Asset specificity

8   The operating levels of the finance function

8.1   Marcus Lintel is employed in the finance function of Everard Co. His duties involve determining the precise unit cost of a range of products manufactured in the company's horticultural division. From time to time, he also prepares reports on variances from the standard cost per unit that he has calculated.

It is clear, therefore, that Marcus is employed by Everard Co in:

- ○   Financial reporting
- ○   Management accounting
- ○   Treasury
- ○   Internal audit

8.2   **Treasury management is NOT concerned with which of the following?**

- ○   Managing cash
- ○   Financial risk management
- ○   Acquiring finance
- ○   Maintaining assets

8.3   **To whom is the internal auditor accountable?**

- ○   The directors of the company
- ○   The employees of the company
- ○   The shareholders of the company
- ○   The external auditors of the company

BPP
LEARNING
MEDIA

8.4 **In relation to variance analysis, which of the following describes the role of the management accountant?**

- ○ Provide management with a list of variances
- ○ Analyse the insights created by the directors to determine the cause of the variance
- ○ Report departments to management when they have adverse variances
- ○ Report variances and the reasons for them to management and assist departments in finding solutions to them

---

8.5 **What is the main focus and role of accounting in the finance function?**

- ○ To pay employee salaries
- ○ To provide information to external auditors
- ○ To record financial information
- ○ To estimate how much to spend on production

8.6 **Which of the following insights would be provided by accountants working in the treasury function?**

- ○ Analysis of the impact of changes to accounting standards on the financial statements
- ○ Reasons for level of performance by monitoring organisational KPIs
- ○ Predictions of demand for new shares at different issue prices to determine an optimum issue price for a new share issue
- ○ Analysis of the effectiveness of internal control systems

---

8.7 **Which of the following insights would be provided by accountants working in the internal audit function?**

- ○ Analysis of the key risks that the organisation faces
- ○ Dashboard of key financial ratios based on draft financial statements
- ○ Master budget based on sub-budgets produced by other functions within the organisation
- ○ Analysis and reporting of working capital

8.8 **Which of the following specialist finance areas helps the organisation to set, monitor and evaluate progress towards achieving organisational goals and objectives?**

- ○ Financial planning and analysis
- ○ Taxation
- ○ Project management
- ○ Project appraisal

8.9 **The time, cost and quality triangle is a key consideration in the work of which of the following specialist areas of finance?**

    ○   Financial planning and analysis

    ○   Taxation

    ○   Project management

    ○   Project appraisal

8.10 Hammerwood Co is under investigation into how it accounts for and calculates VAT.

Which specialist area of finance would liaise with the authorities with regard to the investigation?

    ○   Financial planning and analysis

    ○   Taxation

    ○   Project management

    ○   Project appraisal

8.11 The directors of Forest Co are deciding whether or not to purchase a new information system. To help their decision, they have asked for a professional opinion of the non-financial costs and benefits of the new system.

Which specialist area of finance would provide the directors with the insight they have requested?

    ○   Financial planning and analysis

    ○   Taxation

    ○   Project management

    ○   Project appraisal

8.12 **Which of the following are aspects of strategic partnering for value?**
Select all that apply

    ☐   Basic performance measurement information

    ☐   Expert analysis and insight

    ☐   It is provided to business functions

    ☐   It is provided to the organisation's senior leadership

    ☐   Supporting major strategic decisions

    ☐   Supporting tactical decisions

8.13 **Which of the following is a benefit of strategic partnering for value?**

    ○   Helping business functions to improve their performance

    ○   Ensuring projects are successful

    ○   Ensuring that the senior leadership has the necessary information to make strategic decisions

    ○   Being a trusted advisor to managers of the other business functions

8.14 Who provides the strategic leadership of the finance function?

○ Finance manager

○ Financial controller

○ Finance director

○ Financial reporting manager

8.15 An effective finance team must have an appropriate mix of several attributes.

The overall familiarity and mastery of a particular area is known as:

○ Knowledge

○ Skills

○ Experience

○ Competence

9 The finance function and operations

9.1 Kaizen is a method of quality management that is based on which principle?

○ Elimination of waste

○ Continuous improvement

○ Development of near-perfect products

○ Application of statistics to quality control

9.2 Supply chain partnerships grow out of:

○ Quality accreditation

○ Recognising the supply chain and linkages in a value system

○ An expansion of trade

○ Adopting a marketing philosophy

9.3 Hairdooz Co operates a large chain of hairdressing salons. Peter, a management consultant, has been asked to undertake a review of the company's activities in providing its services to customers. In terms of Porter's value chain, Peter has been asked to focus on the primary activities of the company.

Peter will, therefore, be analysing which of the following?

Select all that apply

☐ Inbound logistics

☐ Procurement

☐ Human resource management

☐ Firm infrastructure

☐ Marketing and sales

☐ Service

9.4 **Porter's value system reflects the value created through the relationship of:**

○ Suppliers, manufacturers, distribution channels and customers' value chains

○ Customers and sales staff

○ Production and sales departments

○ Economy, efficiency and effectiveness in the use of resources

9.5 BCD Co is a large trading company. Steve is the administration manager and is also responsible for legal and compliance functions. Sheila is responsible for after sales service and has responsibility for ensuring that customers who have purchased goods from BCD Co are fully satisfied. Sunny deals with suppliers and negotiates on the price and quality of inventory. He is also responsible for identifying the most appropriate suppliers of plant and machinery for the factory. Sam is the information technology manager and is responsible for all information systems within the company.

According to Porter's value chain, which of the managers is involved in a primary activity?

○ Steve

○ Sheila

○ Sunny

○ Sam

9.6 **A score of six sigma indicates what percentage of manufactured items are within specification?**

○ 93.32%

○ 90%

○ 99.999%

○ 96.66%

9.7 **According to Porter's value chain, the final primary activity is referred to as:**

○ Marketing and sales

○ Outbound logistics

○ Procurement

○ Service

9.8 **Most supply chains involve which of the following?**

○ A number of different companies

○ An organisation's infrastructure

○ After sales service

○ A strategic apex

9.9   **Which of the following best describes 'benchmarking'?**

   ○   Setting and monitoring internal performance standards

   ○   Comparison of actual production against budgeted production

   ○   Comparison of a service, practice or process against one or more similar activities

   ○   Setting a mission statement and ensuring that statement is met over time

9.10   **Inbound logistics is:**

   ○   A secondary activity that refers to price negotiation of incoming raw materials

   ○   A secondary activity that refers to receipt, storage and inward distribution of raw materials

   ○   A primary activity that refers to inbound enquiries and customer complaints

   ○   A primary activity that refers to receipt, storage and inward distribution of raw materials

9.11   **Supplier relationships in a supply network are categorised in which of the following ways?**

   ○   Single, multiple, delegated and parallel

   ○   Primary, secondary and post-purchase

   ○   Phased, pilot and integrated

   ○   One-to-one, several to one, 180 degrees and 360 degrees

9.12   **Which of the following is the main characteristic of a demand network?**

   ○   Products are pushed onto the market by the manufacturer

   ○   Products are developed in response to market signals

   ○   Businesses in the network operate relatively independently

   ○   Interdependence of channel members is reduced

9.13   **Which of the following is NOT one of the four Vs used to analyse the differences between transformational processes?**

   ○   Volume

   ○   Variety

   ○   Velocity

   ○   Visibility

9.14 **What aspect of total quality management (TQM) provides for the participation by selected employees in quality improvement, through meetings to discuss quality-related issues?**

- ○ Work cells
- ○ Continuous improvement
- ○ Quality circles
- ○ Empowerment

9.15 **Which KPI for the operations function measures the proportion of time that a process was actually running compared to what was planned?**

- ○ Operating expense ratio
- ○ Order fulfilment cycle time
- ○ Process downtime level
- ○ Capacity utilisation rate

9.16 **The 5-S model refers to:**

- ○ Internal analysis involving structure, sub-structure, systems, sub-systems and strategy.
- ○ Internal analysis involving style, shared values, skills, staffing and 'soft' information.
- ○ Operations management practices of structurise, systematise, sanitise, standardise and self-discipline.
- ○ The Japanese six-sigma model adapted to Western practice.

9.17 **Which of the following is NOT associated with quality management?**

- ○ 5-S practice
- ○ 180 degree feedback
- ○ Six sigma methodology
- ○ Five-why process

9.18 **The technique PDCA represents:**

- ○ A programme development control activity used in information management
- ○ A framework for bringing about quality improvement to a process or system
- ○ A software inventory system used in warehouse management
- ○ People, developments, controls and appraisal in strategic human resourcing

BPP
LEARNING
MEDIA

9.19 **Optimised production technologies (OPT) is an operations management system which aims to:**

- ○ Improve distribution networks
- ○ Improve supply sourcing alternatives
- ○ Integrate operations and quality assurance
- ○ Reduce production bottlenecks

9.20 **Which of the following statements represents the ultimate aim of total quality management (TQM)?**

- ○ Eliminate the costs of poor quality
- ○ Eliminate all quality-related costs
- ○ Reduce costs of poor quality
- ○ Reduce the workforce

9.21 Mimi has taken on the lead purchasing role in Renford Ltd, a manufacturer of medical suppliers. In her previous role working for a competitor firm, Blyth Ltd, Mimi was instructed to select buyers based upon best price, and value for money. In her new role Mimi is keen to use single suppliers for core components so that Renford's products can be designed to best meet the needs of the market.

Which of the following statements is correct?

- ○ In both of Mimi's roles she favours the collaborative approach
- ○ In her current role Mimi favours a collaborative approach, in her previous role she favoured an adversarial approach
- ○ In her current role Mimi favours an adversarial approach, in her previous role she favoured a collaborative approach
- ○ In both of Mimi's roles she favours the adversarial approach

---

9.22 **The concept of 'zero defects' was championed by which of the following writers on quality?**

- ○ Cousins
- ○ Juran
- ○ Deming
- ○ Crosby

9.23 **Which of the following is NOT a reason why organisations invest in process designs?**

- ○ Increased efficiency
- ○ Increased bureaucracy
- ○ Increased opportunities offered by IT
- ○ Increased competitiveness

---

10 The finance function and sales and marketing

10.1 **A company that concentrates on product features it instinctively believes to be 'right' is referred to as:**

○ A learning organisation

○ Production orientated

○ Product orientated

○ Early stage entrepreneurial

10.2 **Which of the following describes an aspect of marketing rather than selling?**

○ It is concerned with meeting customers' needs for value in the delivery process

○ Customer design is of low importance

○ It is concerned with the satisfaction of customer needs over the long term

○ The stimulation of demand is of low importance

10.3 **'Push' promotion policies involve:**

○ High levels of promotional expenditure to encourage consumers to purchase products

○ Transferring finished goods to intermediaries who then have the task of selling those goods to consumers

○ Using different promotional techniques to influence customer demand in different market segments

○ Using just in time supply policies to meet customer demand

10.4 **A pricing policy designed to establish or increase market share is referred to as:**

○ Penetration pricing

○ Skim pricing

○ Cost-plus pricing

○ Market leader pricing

10.5 **Which of the following shows the correct stages and sequence of the product life cycle?**

○ Product, price, promotion, place

○ Introduction, growth, shakeout, maturity, decline

○ Introduction, growth, middle-age, maturity, decline

○ Product, price, promotion, place, people

10.6 **Direct mailing, branding activities and public relations campaigns are all examples of:**

○ Market process

○ Product placement

○ Promotion

○ Market research

10.7 The Zulon product is manufactured by Arto Co. The product manager for the Zulon is pleased that its dominant market share has been maintained for over five years, but is concerned that market growth has now almost ceased. The product manager does not believe that the product is worthy of any further significant financial support.

In these circumstances and in terms of the BCG Matrix, the product manager should be recommending which of the following strategies?

○ Hold

○ Harvest

○ Divest

○ Build

10.8 **Distribution channels, transport, warehouse and sales outlet locations are all examples of:**

○ 'Place', one component of the marketing mix

○ 'Promotion', one component of the marketing mix

○ 'Physical evidence', one component of the marketing mix

○ The management of operations for a service organisation

10.9 The finance function may interact with the sales and marketing function to help with product costing and pricing.

Which of the following are advantages of marginal cost plus pricing?

Select all that apply

☐ Takes market and demand conditions into account

☐ Simple and easy to use

☐ Ensures fixed costs are covered

☐ Draws management attention to contribution

☐ Ensures all costs are covered in the long term

10.10 **Effective product promotion is centred on:**

○ Production processes

○ Customers and communication

○ Bonuses for sales staff and product quality

○ Effective systems of monitoring and control

10.11 **Which of the following aspects of the marketing mix is NOT relevant to the sale of products?**

- ○ Place
- ○ Promotion
- ○ Processes
- ○ Price

10.12 **What is 'market skimming'?**

- ○ Setting a price based on the cost of the product plus a mark up
- ○ Setting different prices for the same product depending on the market segment
- ○ Setting a relatively low price for a new product
- ○ Setting an initially high price for a new product

10.13 **An approach that encourages individuals to pass on a marketing message through existing social networks is known as:**

- ○ Guerrilla marketing
- ○ Viral marketing
- ○ Experiential marketing
- ○ Cause marketing

10.14 Jane is working on an advertising campaign for her new lawyer's firm. She's decided to work on the anxieties of the public. She is putting together an advert where a child experiences worse and worse conditions until they are eventually living on the street, as a result of their parents' inability to put a proper will in place.

What kind of marketing is Jane doing?

- ○ Relationship
- ○ Experiential
- ○ Post-modern
- ○ Guerrilla

10.15 Ralph Moren, a fashion house, has decided to implement cutting edge IT to support its marketing. It has programmed a robot to search through every image on the internet and, through image recognition software, highlight users that are in photos wearing Ralph Moren clothes. It then intends to use information about these people to inform its next round of marketing.

What type of marketing is Ralph Moren engaged in?

- ○ E-marketing
- ○ Post-modern marketing
- ○ Relationship marketing
- ○ Big data marketing

10.16 The maximisation of customer retention and satisfaction through two-way communication is known as:

- ○ Postmodern marketing
- ○ Experiential marketing
- ○ Relationship marketing
- ○ E-marketing

10.17 Which of the following KPIs used by a sales and marketing function is a measure of the organisation's website's attractiveness?

- ○ Revenue per user
- ○ Upselling success rate
- ○ Conversion rate
- ○ Bounce rate

10.18 Using Ansoff's matrix, how should a business approach introducing a new product to an existing market?

- ○ Market development
- ○ Product development
- ○ Market penetration
- ○ Diversification

10.19 Demand management may be used in the provision and design of a service to ensure that the number of customers matches the available resources to provide the service.

Which of the following is a method of managing demand by charging different customers different prices for the same service?

- ○ Cost reduction
- ○ Price skimming
- ○ Over-booking
- ○ Price discrimination

10.20 **What does the abbreviation B2B mean in a marketing context?**

- ○ Buyer to business
- ○ Bulk to break-up
- ○ Boom to bust
- ○ Business to business

10.21   **Which TWO of the following statements about service companies are correct?**

☐   Service companies deliver a transfer of property to their customers

☐   Service companies have to overcome the issue of homogeneity

☐   Service companies deliver intangible outputs

☐   Service companies must overcome the issue of no storage

☐   Service companies have issues of separation to overcome

10.22   **Travel, luxuries, and home improvements are most likely to be purchased by which segment of the family lifecycle?**

○   Bachelor

○   Full nest (i)

○   Full nest (iii)

○   Empty nest (i)

11   The finance function and human resources

11.1   **Abraham Maslow's theory of motivation is often represented as:**

○   A hierarchy of needs

○   Individual behaviour labelled X or Y

○   A scientific relationship between work and reward

○   A series of negative and a series of positive factors

11.2   **The main weakness of performance related pay is:**

○   There is no attempt to link profits with the pay structure of individuals

○   If targets are not met then employees may become demotivated

○   Employees rarely work harder for additional remuneration

○   It is almost impossible to set appropriate performance targets for manual workers

11.3   **Which of the following is associated with recruitment rather than selection?**

○   Assessment centres

○   Interviews

○   Advertising copy

○   Psychometric testing

BPP
LEARNING
MEDIA

11.4 In the expectancy theory of motivation a person's preference for a particular outcome is referred to as:

○ A valence

○ A hygiene factor

○ A motivator

○ Preference discrimination

11.5 The unwritten expectations that the organisation and the individual have of each other is referred to as:

○ A valence

○ Work/life balance

○ The psychological contract

○ Expectation management

11.6 Which of the following describes a psychological contract?

○ The intangible benefits arising from outsourcing

○ The responsibilities of a member of society to their country

○ The mutual expectations of an employee and employer

○ The use of expert systems in the psychometric testing of new recruits

11.7 Which of the following are potential advantages of self-appraisals?
Select all that apply

☐ Subordinates tend to know their superior better than superiors know their subordinates

☐ People are often not the best judges of their own performance

☐ It saves the manager time

☐ Increases the managerial role in appraisal

☐ Offers increased responsibility to the individual

11.8 Which of the equations below represents Victor Vroom's model of motivation (Force may sometimes be replaced by Motivation in this equation)?

○ Force × Valence = Expectation

○ Force × Expectation = Subjective probability

○ Subjective probability × Expectation = Force

○ Force = Valence × Expectation

11.9 **Motivation theories and reward systems derived from F W Taylor's thinking are by nature best described as:**

○ Behavioural

○ Human relations

○ Content

○ Scientific

11.10 **Enlargement, enrichment and rotation are terms associated with which of the following?**

○ Adjustments to an individual's job content and role

○ Improvements brought about by competitive benchmarking

○ Market and product development strategies

○ Customer approval ratings

11.11 **Which of the following is unlikely to be a feature of a successful incentive scheme?**

○ Profit sharing

○ A clear link between performance and reward

○ Significant influence by uncontrollable factors

○ Key results are identified and specified in detail

11.12 **An 'assessment centre' approach is used:**

○ As part of an appraisal process

○ As part of a process of training and development

○ As part of a selection process

○ As part of an exit interview process

11.13 **Job rotation involves:**

○ A redesign of a person's post based upon job analysis

○ The movement of an individual to another post in order to gain experience

○ The expansion and enrichment of a person's job content

○ The relocation of a post holder in order to benefit from the experience of a number of potential mentors

11.14 **360 degree feedback is part of a system that encourages:**

○ Organisational appraisal based on feedback from customers and suppliers

○ Organisational appraisal based on relative industry and competitor performance

○ Performance appraisal based on feedback from peers, subordinates, line managers and even external parties

○ Personal appraisal based on line manager feedback and self-appraisal documentation

11.15 **Recruitment involves:**

- ○ Advertising a vacancy and interviewing
- ○ Conducting interviews and tests
- ○ Advertising a vacancy and initial screening of candidates
- ○ Ensuring that contract negotiation complies with organisational policy

---

11.16 **Which of the following KPIs for the human resources function measures staff retention?**

- ○ Employee churn rate
- ○ Employee engagement level
- ○ Employee satisfaction index
- ○ Time to hire

11.17 **Intelligence, aptitudes and disposition are often factors identified in:**

- ○ A job description
- ○ Appraisal targets
- ○ A person specification
- ○ 360 degree documentation

11.18 **Which of the following is the factor that Taylor believed would be most effective in motivating workers?**

- ○ Remuneration levels
- ○ Job security
- ○ Good working conditions
- ○ Minimal supervision

11.19 **Which of the following describes an organisation's training gap?**

- ○ The difference between its current level of training and the level of training it aspires to
- ○ The difference between the knowledge and skills that it has and the knowledge and skills that it wants
- ○ The difference between the knowledge and skills that it wants and the knowledge and skills that it needs
- ○ The difference between the number of skilled and unskilled workers

---

11.20 **Ensuring that an organisation has suitable replacements available to take over positions as they become available is known as:**

○ Career management

○ Human resource development

○ Performance management

○ Succession planning

11.21 Fernando is concerned about the levels of motivation amongst his workforce. Having consulted with some long-serving employees he is thinking of offering his staff the choice of working longer, but fewer days each week.

Which form of flexible working is Fernando considering?

○ Flexitime

○ Shift system

○ Compressed week

○ Part-time

12 The finance function and IT

12.1 **Which of the following is NOT an advantage that virtual companies have?**

○ Materials can be acquired more cheaply

○ It can respond to the environment quickly

○ It has a low cost base

○ It has a single supply chain

12.2 **Virtual teams are normally a result of:**

○ An economic downturn

○ Developments in technology and information systems

○ Poor staff morale and motivation within the workforce

○ Ineffective human resourcing practices

12.3 The use of computer-integrated manufacturing (CIM) is an example of how technology has enabled change.

Which of the following describes how CIM has enabled change?

○ By changing the type of products that are made

○ By changing the way in which products are made

○ By changing how employees are mobilised

○ By changing how services are provided

12.4 A software management system combining all of a globally diverse organisation's sales, marketing and customer support information is known as:

○ Distributed data processing (DDP)

○ Customer relationship management (CRM)

○ A database management system (DBMS)

○ A wide area network (WAN)

12.5 A system that simulates the problem solving techniques of human experts is known as:

○ An expert system

○ A knowledge transfer programme

○ A smart system

○ A management information system

12.6 Which of the following is an example of a development cost of a system?

○ Purchasing a new building to house the system

○ Fitting wiring and air-conditioning units where the system is to be located

○ Measuring and analysing the existing system

○ Staff training on the new system

12.7 Office automation systems (OAS) are computer systems designed to increase the productivity of data and information workers.

Which of the following is an example of an OAS?

○ Digital filing systems

○ Computer aided design (CAD)

○ Computer aided manufacturing (CAM)

○ Specialised financial software that analyses trading situations

12.8 Executive information systems (EIS) and expert systems (ES) are examples of:

○ Customer relationship management software

○ Database management systems

○ Computer networking

○ Decision based software

12.9 A high figure on which of the following KPIs for the IT function indicates the possibility of an IT hardware failure in the near future?

○ Help desk first call resolution

○ Average age of IT infrastructure

○ IT project cost variance

○ Number of IT security breaches

12.10   Which of the following does NOT represent a control in a computer network?

     ○   A firewall

     ○   Internet gateways

     ○   Passwords

     ○   A cookie

12.11   An expert system describes:

     ○   A database built upon past knowledge and experience

     ○   A powerful off the shelf software solution

     ○   An online library of operating advice and handy hints

     ○   An electronic version of working papers assembled by the Research and Development department

12.12   A lack of physical presence and extensive use of IT are typical features of which sort of organisation?

     ○   Non-governmental organisations (NGO)

     ○   Multinational enterprises (MNE)

     ○   Shamrock organisations

     ○   Virtual organisations

12.13   Which type of security risk involves overloading an internet site with traffic?

     ○   Worms

     ○   Trojan horses

     ○   Denial of service attacks

     ○   Hacking

12.14   Local area networking is used for:

     ○   Communication between computers within a limited geographical area

     ○   Structuring an organisation within a division or business unit

     ○   Exchange of information through a trade association or region

     ○   Managing a complex operational issue via a global interface with trade associations and professional bodies

12.15   Which of the following is a system that is designed to co-ordinate all of an organisation's functions, resources and information?

     ○   A knowledge management system

     ○   A customer relationship system

     ○   An expert system

     ○   An enterprise-wide system

BPP
LEARNING
MEDIA

12.16   **Which method of system changeover carries the highest risk?**

○   Direct changeover

○   Parallel running

○   Pilot operation

○   Phased or modular changeover

12.17   **Selecting one part or several parts of an organisation to operate a new system in conjunction with the existing system is known as:**

○   Phased or modular changeover

○   Parallel running

○   Direct changeover

○   Pilot operation

12.18   Megan works as a research scientist, and during one experiment accidently created a new form of water-resistant but breathable fabric. Unfortunately, Megan did not grasp the significance of her discovery, so her sample, and the details of her experiment are sitting in her company's archives.

Which of the following best describes the situation outlined above?

○   Megan has created new data

○   Megan has created tacit knowledge

○   Megan has created information

○   Megan has created explicit knowledge

Answers to objective test questions

1 Role of the finance function

1.1 The correct answer is: A code for organisational direction, administration and control.

Corporate governance refers to how organisations are directed and controlled.

1.2 The correct answer is: Creating the maximum output for minimum input.

Effective business processes create the maximum output for the minimum input. Quality and value for money are not relevant for effectiveness.

1.3 The correct answer is: Primary objective.

A business is a profit-seeking organisation. The importance of profit may not be apparent from the organisation's vision and mission because these focus on the general purpose and direction of the organisation.

A primary objective of a business would be to generate or increase profits – so this would differentiate a business from a not for profit organisation. Secondary objectives are driven by primary objectives. They may not indicate a business because a not for profit organisation may have similar secondary objectives to a profit seeking one (eg reduce staff costs).

1.4 The correct answer is: Making profits.

Non-governmental organisations are organisations that pursue activities for the good of society, such as protecting the environment, providing basic social services or undertaking community development work. They are generally not profit-oriented.

1.5 The correct answer is: Efficient use of resources.

Public sector organisations aim to use their resources efficiently. Profits and losses are not the main concerns of these organisations because they seek to provide public services. Charitable donations are not an objective of public sector organisations.

1.6 The correct answer is: Economic.

This is the responsibility to the shareholder and other directly linked parties to keep the costs of the company low.

Although you could argue that the company is also following the letter of the law, and fulfilling its legal responsibility, the fact that many countries alter laws to stop this kind of action shows that it is more comfortably part of the economic responsibility.

The ethical and philanthropic responsibilities are more about giving time or money to things that society wants. This would not cover tax avoidance.

1.7 The correct answer is: Mutual organisations.

Mutuals are primarily in business to provide services to their customers. They are not owned by shareholders who they have to pay a share of their profit to.

1.8 The correct answer is: The chairman and chief executive are different individuals in order to prevent one person having too much power within the company.

It is good corporate governance to reduce the power any one individual has in a company and therefore it is important to separate the roles of chairman and chief executive. There is no reason why a chairman cannot hold other directorships, providing this does not breach any other corporate governance rules.

1.9 The correct answer is: Time available to devote to the role.

This is a major problem for non-executive directors, because they are likely to have other commitments. You should have had to think through the other options, however. Some of the advantages of non-executive directors are that they offer a comfort factor for third parties such as investors and suppliers; they have a wider perspective and (hopefully) no vested interest; and they have a combination of knowledge/expertise and detachment.

1.10 The correct answers are:

- Faster and easier communication
- Changes to who competitors and stakeholders are.

A third consequence is increasing (not reduced) levels of competition. It does not increase the power of stakeholders (it may increase or decrease power, depending on the stakeholder) and it makes the rules of business more (not less) dynamic.

1.11 The correct answer is: It should be independent of management actions.

Written codes of ethics set out values, not attitudes to risk. They should be independent of management actions. Non-compliance should not be supported and they are based on ethics not law.

1.12 The correct answer is:

| Encourages new entrants | Erects a barrier to new entrants |
| Low competition | High capital costs |

Low levels of competition in an industry make it more attractive for new entrants. High capital costs involve risk and fundraising challenges which can act as a barrier to new entrants.

1.13 The correct answer is: Threat of new entrants.

The marketing tactic of making key accessories unique to a particular product discourages competitors from offering substitute products because the costs of doing so will be greater and entry into the market made more difficult. It does not alter the balance of power of suppliers or customers nor affect the intensity of competitive rivalry.

1.14 The correct answer is: An increasingly prominent role for non-executive directors.

Non-executive directors should provide a balancing influence and play a key role in reducing conflicts of interest between management and shareholders.

1.15 The correct answer is: Data integrity.

Data integrity concerns the finance function acting as a trusted source of management information.

1.16 The correct answer is: I, II, III and IV.

Recycling reduces the amount of waste the business produces. Energy efficiency reduces the amount of energy it needs and therefore the amount of pollution caused. Careful selection of suppliers (for example those that are environmentally friendly) helps reduce its impact as well. Buying raw materials locally means that less pollution is used in transporting the goods.

1.17 The correct answers are:

- Integrity
- Professional competence and due care

Darlene is considering misleading the client because she is not fully CIMA qualified and working beyond her competence.

1.18 The correct answer is: A framework of fundamental principles.

CIMA's Code of Ethics for professional accountants is based on a framework of fundamental principles.

1.19 The correct answer is: Planning and forecasting.

Planning and forecasting involves taking an organisation's strategic goals and critical success factors and turning them into a detailed roadmap from where the organisation is to where it wants to be.

1.20 The correct answer is: To provide guidance on the standards of best practice that companies should adopt.

Codes of practice are usually associated with a principles-based approach (rather than a rules-based approach). The words 'guidance' and 'should adopt' were the key words to lead to the correct option.

2 Activities of finance professionals

2.1 The correct answer is: Treat this stakeholder as a key player when formulating future strategies.

The scenario suggests that the stakeholder has high power (ability to close down operations) and high influence (considerable influence is stated) and therefore, according to Mendelow, they should be treated as a key player.

2.2 The correct answers are:

- Accounting skills
- Analytical skills
- Business understanding.

Commercial curiosity and passion for business are part of the contribute insights into drivers of cost, risk and value skillset. Preparedness to challenge is part of the effective business partnering relationships skillset.

2.3 The correct answer is: Financial data.

Financial data consists of standard metrics which are well tracked and understood by an organisation. Enterprise and big data contain financial data, but with additional data added on in terms of scale and complexity.

2.4 The correct answer is: Environmental scanning.

Gathering external data from a range of sources is known as environmental scanning. It may be a formal method of data collection, and an example might be market research, but environmental scanning is wider in scope than that.

2.5 The correct answers are:

- Owners of small businesses may lose control of the organisation when it grows and it becomes necessary to appoint managers to run the business – owners of the business lose control to management.

- The financial independence of an organisation may be reduced when additional shares or loans are required – the interest of existing shareholders is affected by giving rights to new shareholders or loan providers.

The other options only affect one set of stakeholders – the business's management – therefore there is no conflict.

2.6 The correct answers are:

- Shareholders
- Bankers

Return on investment will be of greatest importance to the shareholders and bankers – both of which have a financial interest in the company.

2.7 The correct answer is: Data cleansing.

Identifying inaccuracies in data and modifying or deleting them is known as data cleansing.

2.8   The correct answer is: Insights are indications of the drivers of value for an organisation.

Insights are more than reporting of basic financial information; they are indications of the drivers of value for the organisation. When finance professionals report insights, they use them to explain the reasons why the organisation's performance was as reported, what is happening to the business now and what might happen in the future. This means that insights enable advice to be provided that can influence potential business solutions and subsequently impact business decisions.

2.9   The correct answer is: Analysis.

The four levels of data analysis ask the following questions:

Reporting – 'What has happened?'

Analysis – 'Why did it happen?'

Monitoring – 'What is happening now?'

Prediction – 'What might happen?'

2.10   The correct answer is: A manager.

The others are known as connected stakeholders.

2.11   The correct answer is: Format.

The format of a communication considers how and where the communication is received by the stakeholder.

2.12   The correct answer is: Business partnering.

Finance functions embedding themselves and working alongside different business areas, rather than just being a separate business function, is known as business partnering. Strategic partnering for value involves the finance function providing strategic advice and insights to an organisation's senior leadership.

Segregation involves parts of the finance function being separated into a shared service centre and outsourcing involves a third party taking over a particular function of the business.

2.13   The correct answers are:

- Budgeting
- Information systems

Finance develops budgets for business areas which are linked via a master budget for the organisation. It also works with those charged with developing and maintaining the organisation's information systems (which themselves connect business areas) to ensure that its requirements for data and information to create insights are met.

Appraisal systems come under the control of HR. Process design is a role of operations and target marketing is a role of sales and marketing.

2.14   The correct answers are:

- Empathy with business
- Compelling communication
- Preparedness to challenge

Analytical skills are part of the ability to integrate, apply and communicate skillset. Commercial curiosity and professional objectivity are part of the contribute insights into drivers of cost, risk and value skillset.

2.15   The correct answer is: Information should have a value greater than the cost of obtaining it

All information has a value (for example, the value of the benefits it brings to an organisation). It is important that information is cost effective and so the value should not exceed the costs of obtaining it. This includes the time users spend working out what the information means. Therefore, it is important that information is clear and easy to understand if it is to be produced effectively.

3 Technologies used in business and finance

3.1 The correct answer is: Cloud service.

This is an on-demand service being driven by equipment run by a third party. This company is offering cloud computing. A WAN would be a wide network within an organisation. Similarly, grid computing is when assets within the company are being used, although apart from that it describes this situation very well. The system is acting somewhat as an ES, because it is creating easy outputs, but the relationship is still best described by cloud computing.

3.2 The correct answer is: Digital technology.

It is digital technology that is powering the fourth industrial revolution. The other options powered the third industrial revolution.

3.3 The correct answer is: Big data analytics relies on digital information.

Information may be written, verbal or confidential, but if it is not digitised it cannot be analysed by big data analytics.

3.4 The correct answer is: Big data analytics shifts organisational focus from individual customers to groups of customers.

Big data analytics enables greater focus on individual customers. The other options are all correct statements about big data analytics.

3.5 The correct answer is: Effect.

The statement describes the effect of the fourth industrial revolution. Velocity refers to speed of change and scope refers to the depth of change within industries. Application is not a feature of the fourth industrial revolution.

3.6 The correct answer is: Volume.

The volume of data generated is a key feature of 'big data'. Volume is one of the four V's along with veracity, velocity and variety.

3.7 The correct answers are:

- Jobs being replaced by automation
- Greater customer expectations for products and services provided

These are changes and dynamics of the fourth industrial revolution. The opposite of the other options is true. Transport and communication costs are falling, there are more opportunities to enhance existing products (with digital capabilities) and there is more scope for collaboration and innovation between businesses.

3.8 The correct answer is: Process automation

The ability of systems to perform routine activities without the input of a human is known as process automation.

3.9 The correct answer is: Artificial intelligence.

The ability of a computer system to assist a human operator to make decisions and solve problems is known as artificial intelligence.

3.10 The correct answer is: Waterfall charts.

Waterfall charts are often used to present variance analysis and are designed so that the eye focuses on the most significant movements first.

3.11 The correct answer is: Dashboards.

Dashboards provide a summary of four or five relevant drivers that give an overview of a business area.

3.12 The correct answer is: Propagation.

Propagation refers to the fact that there are many copies of a blockchain ledger, but no master copy. Permanence is the fact that the blockchain cannot be deleted and programmability means that program code can be added to the transaction information.

3.13 The correct answer is: Past transactions on a blockchain can only be edited with the consent of the majority of other holders of the same blockchain.

This option describes the feature of permanence. There is no master copy of a blockchain. New transactions can be added to a blockchain and one potential use of blockchain is the creation of smart-contracts.

3.14 The correct answer is: Mobile technology.

SMS and MMS are early examples of the use of mobile technology.

3.15 The correct answer is: Internet of things.

Devices that can transfer data over the internet without requiring human-to-human or human-to-computer interaction are known as the internet of things.

4 Digital technologies and the finance function

4.1 The correct answer is: Management accounting.

Management accounting involves analysing data to provide information that will be used as the basis of a management decision.

4.2 The correct answer is: Verifying the ownership of assets.

Distributed ledgers can be used by the financial reporting team to verify the ownership of assets.

4.3 The correct answer is: Treasury.

The interest rate is the price of money. A rise in interest rates will raise the price of borrowing, and increase the interest that can be made on surplus funds. Both of these areas are covered by a treasury team.

4.4 The correct answer is: Internal audit

Internal audit has responsibility for ensuring that the organisation's rules and policies are complied with.

4.5 The correct answer is: Creation of statutory accounts.

Creation of statutory accounts is a role of the financial reporting section that can be automated.

Calculation of variances is a role of the management accounting function. Investment appraisal calculations are performed by treasury and monitoring transactions is a role of internal audit.

4.6 The correct answers are:

- Simulations of cyberattacks to test IT controls
- Vulnerability testing to identify weaknesses in the business

Both of these impacts involve testing of controls to determine weaknesses in the organisation and are roles of the internal audit team.

Cashflow forecasting is a role of treasury, downloading bank transactions is performed by financial reporting and budgeting is performed by management accounting.

4.7 The correct answer is: A management accountant.

Management accountants provide information for management such as cost accounting, budgets and budgetary control.

Financial reporting accountants are responsible for routine accounting, accounting reports, cashiers' duties and cash control.

A treasurer would be responsible for treasury management: raising and investing funds and cash flow control.

The finance director approves the budget.

4.8 The correct answer is: Financial reporting.

The FRC and IASB are involved in financial reporting.

4.9 The correct answers are:

- Dealing with complexity
- Working in a creative and agile way

The other key aspect is lifelong learning (not learning something for life).

4.10 The correct answers are:

- Arranging finance
- Management of foreign currency holdings
- 'What if' scenario planning for investment appraisal

Variance analysis is associated with management accounting. Financial accounting ratios and asset revaluations are the responsibility of the financial reporting accountants.

4.11 The correct answer is: Data held must be adequate, relevant and not excessive.

This statement describes the principle of data minimisation.

Data can only be held for valid reasons, individuals must be notified of the purpose when the data is first collected and organisations must always correct inaccurate or misleading data.

4.12 The correct answer is: There is application of knowledge across a range of different tasks.

This type of activity is suited to human-only processing. Routine processing is best suited to machine-only processing even if errors might arise that need a human to resolve. Human and machine hybrid activities are suited to where technology can augment human intelligence.

4.13 The correct answer is: The increasing use of fraud detection systems in e-commerce.

The use of fraud detection systems does not raise ethical issues because they are used to prevent criminal offences. If individuals obey the law then they have nothing to fear from them.

Increasing computing power means that more information is held about individuals than ever before. Falling costs of storage and ease of transfer mean that data is collected, moved and stored more regularly and is open to intrusion, putting the privacy and security of individuals at risk.

4.14 The correct answers are:

- Data visualisation
- Mobile technology

The insights are viewed (using data visualisation) on a tablet away from the office (using mobile technology).

4.15 The correct answer is: Evaluation

The other options are all rights granted to individuals by data protection legislation.

BPP
LEARNING
MEDIA

4.16   The correct answers are: Responsibility, Motivation and Telling.

The CRUMPET acronym is useful for remembering the advantages of the budget process:

- Co-ordination – Budgets help managers to organise their departments by ensuring that the work efforts undertaken are consistent in helping the organisation to achieve its objectives.

- Responsibility – Budgets provide the organisation's managers with authority to undertake expenditure in accordance with wider organisational plans.

- Utilisation – Budgets help to ensure that managers have better visibility over the resources that they are responsible for using.

- Motivation – Budgets, if set appropriately, can have a motivating effect on managers as they may be more inclined to work within the budgets that have been set for them.

- Planning – Budgets help to focus the attention of managers as they require them to be forward-looking in terms of how best to use the resources that they have been allocated, considering relevant opportunities and threats.

- Evaluation – Budgets provide a helpful point of reference during the process of assessing the performance the manager responsible for that budget.

- Telling – Budgets are a useful communication tool as they set out the expectations of the organisation in terms of the level of performance that managers are required to deliver over a period of time.

4.17   The correct answer is: Increased material costs.

A more aggressive policy will see payments to suppliers being delayed. This may result in the loss of prompt payment discounts or higher prices.

Aggressive policies will see inventory holdings reduced, so obsolesce should fall. Credit periods to customers will be reduced, potentially reducing sales, and hence bad and doubtful debts should also fall.

4.18   The correct answer is: Reviewing the effectiveness of risk management procedures.

Roles that come within the scope of internal audit include:

- Reviewing internal controls, risk management systems and financial reports

- Managing the data used by management to identify risks

- Identifying methods for prioritising and managing risks

- Reporting on how effective risk management controls are

- Prevention and detection of fraud and intentional misstatements in financial statements

Whilst internal auditors should ideally act independently this is not a function of the scope of their work. Opinions on the truth and fairness of the financial statements are given by the external auditors. The audit committee reviews the effectiveness of the IA department.

4.19   The correct answers are: Staff not taking holiday, and the lavish lifestyles of staff, not in keeping with their salary.

The symptoms of fraud include:

- Staff not taking leave or holiday – may be a sign that staff do not want others to find out what they have been doing

- Strange transactions – for example, cash payments to staff or transfers to unnamed bank accounts may be a sign that the transaction is fraudulent

- Payments being made out of proportion to work done – this may be a sign of fraud

- Lavish lifestyles of employees – staff living beyond their means may mean they are defrauding the company, or may need to do so in future if their funds run out

Low staff morale, domination by powerful staff members, and complex corporate structures are causes of fraud, rather than symptoms.

4.20   The correct answer is: Threat to independence.

As the audit committee oversees the work of the IA department the appointment of Molly's father will threaten her independence.

Organisational constraints refer to the difficulty in smaller firms in adequately segregated the IA department from other functions. Molly has three years' experience, and there is no information to cast doubt on her qualifications or experience. The self-interest threat would arise if Molly, or the IA department started to act in their own interests rather than Theta's.

4.21   The correct answer is: Tax evasion.

Tax evasion is illegal and involves reducing tax liability by breaking the law. For example, by deliberately understanding profits.

4.22   The correct answer is: Tax mitigation.

Tax mitigation involves reducing tax liability through conduct that does not frustrate the intentions of Parliament when the law was created.

5   Data and the finance function

5.1   The correct answer is: Cloud computing.

Cloud computing allows a single data source to be maintained and shared by multiple users.

5.2   The correct answer is: Sales and marketing.

Customer preferences and what can add value to the customer are relevant to an organisation's sales and marketing.

5.3   The correct answer is: To create value.

The creation of value is the key strategic objective of the majority of organisations. A better understanding of customer needs allows products and services to be designed that add value for them.

5.4   The correct answer is: Data visualisation.

Data visualisation tools improve the communication of information, making it more effective and rich.

5.5   The correct answer is: 3-D printing.

3-D printing allows the fast assembly of prototype products. Changes can be made quickly and sent to any business location that has a 3-D printer.

5.6   The correct answers are:

• Responses from online promotions, advertising and emails
• Tablet and phone apps

The other options are sources of operational, not customer, data.

5.7   The correct answer is: Operations.

Reverse logistics systems are found in the operations function (just like logistics systems).

5.8   The correct answer is: Mobile technology.

Mobile technology allows decision makers (and anyone) to access information provided they have access to a phone signal.

5.9   The correct answers are:

• Inventory management systems
• Quality control systems
• Manufacturing resource planning systems

The other options are sources of customer (sales and marketing) data.

5.10   The correct answer is: Data analytics.

Big data might contain the patterns or trends, and data visualisation helps to communicate them, but it is data analytics that actually identifies them.

5.11   The correct answer is: High levels of rework.

Quality control systems help to identify products or processes with high levels of rework or wastage. Slow moving product lines would be indicated by inventory management systems. Delays in transferring documents would be identified by electronic data interchange systems. Poor working capital management would be identified from the financial systems.

5.12   The correct answer is: Digital assets' ownership rights usually require specific protection.

Digital assets are a form of intangible asset. They are permanent and the ease with which they can be copied means that owners of digital assets must take steps to protect their ownership rights. Users are normally granted a licence to use the asset only.

5.13   The correct answer is: The organisation is vulnerable to errors and poor quality data.

If organisations are increasingly dependent on data it makes them more vulnerable to errors and poor quality data.

5.14   The correct answers are:

- To be informed
- Access
- Restrict processing

The other options are not rights granted under the Data Protection Act 2018.

5.15   The correct answer is: Transparency.

As organisations use more data, it is important that they are transparent with individuals about why data about them is collected and the purposes it is put to.

6   Using data to create and preserve value

6.1   The correct answer is: Sensor.

In terms of a feedback system, a sensor is a measuring or recording device.

6.2   The correct answer is: Purchase of information regarding the business environment.

An information gap is where an organisation's existing systems do not provide information that is required. In this case, it is the operations system that contains the information gap. Suitable methods to close the gap would be to reconfigure the existing systems to provide the information required, to purchase an entirely new system or to develop new parts for the existing system.

Purchasing information regarding the business environment might close an information gap (for example with regard to sales and marketing), but it won't close a gap in an internal system such as an operations system.

6.3   The correct answers are:

- Real time access
- Dashboards

Real time access, reports and dashboards and web are found at the top of a business intelligence stack.

6.4   The correct answer is: Extraction.

In terms of Data ETL systems, 'E' refers to extraction, 'T' refers to transformation and 'L' refers to loading.

6.5   The correct answer is: Comparator.

In terms of a feedback system, a comparator compares an actual result against a plan or standard.

6.6   The correct answer is: Transformed data is written into a target database.

During the 'load' phase, transformed data is written into a target database.

6.7   The correct answer is: Online analytical processing, data mining, query and reporting systems

Online analytical processing, data mining, query and reporting systems allow managers without specialist IT or analytical expertise to drill into and view data in different ways to identify hidden relationships.

6.8   The correct answer is: Warehouse management.

In a business intelligence stack, data storage is provided by metadata, data warehouses and warehouse management.

6.9   The correct answer is: An effector.

Effectors act on a comparison by the comparator, based on information from a sensor. Rohan does not work at a high enough level within the organisation to be known as a higher-level controller.

6.10   The correct answer is: IT infrastructure.

An organisation's IT infrastructure is found at the very bottom of its business intelligence stack.

6.11   The correct answer is: Speculative model.

The three stages of data modelling are conceptual model, logical model and physical model.

6.12   The correct answer is: Reorganising or transforming data to make it easier to read or more meaningful.

Data manipulation involves reorganising or transforming data to make it easier to read or more meaningful.

6.13   The correct answer is: Exploratory data analysis.

Exploratory data analysis involves finding new relationships or features in a data set. Confirmatory data analysis involves confirming or disproving an hypothesis. Predictive data analysis involves making forecasts based on techniques such as statistical modelling. Text data analysis involves extracting and classifying data from textual sources.

6.14   The correct answer is: Confirmatory data analysis.

Exploratory data analysis involves finding new relationships or features in a data set. Confirmatory data analysis involves proving or disproving an hypothesis. Predictive data analysis involves making forecasts based on techniques such as statistical modelling. Text data analysis involves extracting and classifying data from textual sources.

6.15   The correct answer is: Veracity.

Veracity relates to the trustworthiness of data, something that can be improved by data cleansing.

7 Structure and shape of the finance function

7.1 The correct answer is: Strategic alliance.

Strategic alliances are simply agreements between parties. The company's plan is not a joint venture because no separate company is being formed. It is not licensing because the other party will not be manufacturing a product or using a brand name. It is not outsourcing because no activities are being relocated.

7.2 The correct answers are:

- Creating and communicating insights
- Analysing information that has often been generated automatically

The other options are roles that were traditionally performed by the finance function which are now often automated.

7.3 The correct answer is: Matrix.

In a matrix structure an employee may report to a line manager as well as a product or project manager. This encourages employee flexibility and multiple reporting.

7.4 The correct answer is: Shared service centres.

Segregation is caused by parts of the finance function being moved to shared service centres.

7.5 The correct answer is: Outsource partners.

Mintzberg's organisation includes: the operating core, technostructure, middle line, strategic apex and support staff.

7.6 The correct answer is: Tailored response.

By centralising the finance function of a company to a single location efficiencies are improved. This may lead to reduction in headcount and pooling of knowledge. However, the local finance team may have been able to understand local requirements better.

7.7 The correct answer is: Process automation

Process automation has meant that fewer staff are required at the bottom of the finance function's hierarchy to process transactions.

7.8 The correct answer is: II and IV.

Outsourcing functions like IT simplifies the structure of an organisation and reduces ongoing operational costs, but because support is external to the organisation, there may be a greater lead time required for resolving IT issues. Because there is less direct control over subcontractor's employees, long-term projects, in particular, may be prone to disruption.

7.9 The correct answer is: An outsourced IT function.

Where an organisation outsources its IT function, it becomes the client and the outsourcing partner becomes the vendor.

7.10 The correct answer is: Outsourcing.

Service level agreements (SLAs) are contractual agreements negotiated between an organisation and another organisation to which it is outsourcing an aspect of its operations. The purpose of the SLA is to specify the level of service that the external organisation is required to provide.

7.11 The correct answer is: The organisation can achieve economies of scale.

In a functional structure, groups of workers are created that focus on one activity. This focus of resources enables economies of scale to be achieved. Because it involves a strict hierarchy, problems of hierarchy are not prevented.

The strict structure does not facilitate cross-functional co-ordination or innovation. Both require a looser type of structure.

7.12 The correct answer is: Strict contractual control over the business partner.

Alliance agreements are looser than joint-venture agreements with less control over the business partner and are easier to break.

The other options are all benefits of an alliance.

7.13 The correct answer is: Line of command.

Scalar chain refers to an organisation's line of command.

7.14 The correct answer is: Offshoring.

Offshoring means moving work to another country ('off shore'). Outsourcing to another country is an example of offshoring, but the term also refers to moving some of an organisation's own operations to another country.

7.15 The correct answer is: Outsourcing carries commercial and reputational risks.

There are several risks associated with outsourcing: being locked in to an unsatisfactory relationship; losing in-house assets and knowledge; sharing confidential information; and 'reputational' risk (if the supplier gives poor service, or is found to be unethical in its practices, say).

The other statements are untrue: an organisation should not outsource its 'core competences' (areas of unique and non-replicable competitive advantage); outsourcing often creates economies of scale (taking advantage of the larger dedicated resources of the contractor); and outsourcing still incurs significant costs, including internal costs of managing the relationship.

7.16 The correct answer is: Physical asset specificity.

Physical asset specificity refers to customised assets, or those with limited other uses, and thus have lower alternative use values. This means they are more specific to the task, as in the case of needing to build this lathe.

Human asset specificity refers to workers acquiring knowledge or skills that are specific to their role. This knowledge or skill has a higher value within the activity (and therefore within an organisation) rather than outside it.

Temporal specificity refers to activities involving perishable goods, that are so time specific that an alternative processor is unlikely to be found in time if the current supplier fails.

Site specificity refers to certain sites, such as factories, that are immobile and therefore specific to a certain location.

7.17 The correct answer is: Standardisation.

Williamson (1981) identified three aspects to the make or buy decision:

- Uncertainty – Uncertainty in the business environment makes it difficult to arrange long-term contracts and therefore it is more likely for a process to be undertaken in-house.

- Frequency – Work is more likely to be outsourced if it is infrequent or unlikely to reoccur.

- Asset specificity – Where the assets required are specific to the transaction, then the process should be taken on in-house as the corresponding transaction costs will be high.

Whether products are standard or non-standard is a consideration in TCT as it impacts upon transaction costs, however, it is not a specific element of Williamson's make or buy decision.

8 The operating levels of the finance function

8.1 The correct answer is: Management accounting.

Cost accounting and variance analysis are both elements of management accounting.

8.2 The correct answer is: Maintaining assets.

Treasury management is concerned with aspects such as managing cash and financial risk and acquiring finance. The maintenance of assets is the responsibility of the department that owns them.

8.3 The correct answer is: The directors of the company.

The internal auditor is an employee of the company whose duties are fixed by (and therefore they report to) the company's management – the directors.

8.4 The correct answer is: Report variances and the reasons for them to management and assist departments in finding solutions to them.

As well as reporting variances to management, the management accountant has a role to play in supporting business functions in finding solutions to them. They create insights and pass them up the organisation's hierarchy, possibly to the directors.

8.5 The correct answer is: To record financial information.

This is its basic, original role and is still the best way to describe its part in the modern business organisation.

8.6 The correct answer is: Predictions of demand for new shares at different issue prices to determine an optimum issue price for a new share issue.

The treasury function is involved in sourcing new finance, such as new share issues. Therefore, an insight provided would be with regard to determining an issue price for a new share issue.

8.7 The correct answer is: Analysis of the key risks that the organisation faces.

The internal audit function is concerned with internal control systems, and the management of the key risks the organisation faces.

8.8 The correct answer is: Financial planning and analysis.

It is the financial planning and analysis team that helps the organisation to set, monitor and evaluate progress towards achieving organisational goals and objectives.

8.9 The correct answer is: Project management.

Project management teams work to deliver projects within a timeframe, of the correct quality and within budget.

8.10 The correct answer is: Taxation.

The organisation's taxation team would liaise with the tax authorities regarding the VAT investigation.

8.11 The correct answer is: Project appraisal.

Costs and benefits of a new project would be provided by the project appraisal team.

8.12 The correct answers are:

- Expert analysis and insight
- It is provided to the organisation's senior leadership
- Supporting major strategic decisions

Strategic partnering for value involves accountants providing expert analysis and insight to the organisation's senior leadership to help support major strategic decisions. The other options are aspects of business partnering.

8.13   The correct answer is: Ensuring that the senior leadership has the necessary information to make strategic decisions.

Strategic partnering for value involves providing insights to the senior leadership of the organisation to help them make major strategic decisions. Supporting other business functions is a benefit of business partnering.

8.14   The correct answer is: Finance director.

It is the finance director (or chief financial officer) that provides the strategic leadership of the finance function.

8.15   The correct answer is: Experience.

The overall familiarity and mastery of a particular area is known as experience.

9   The finance function and operations

9.1   The correct answer is: Continuous improvement

Kaizen is based on the principle of continuous improvement.

Elimination of waste is a principle of TQM. Developing near-perfect products is a principle of six sigma. Application of statistics to quality control is a principle of statistical process control.

9.2   The correct answer is: Recognising the supply chain and linkages in a value system.

Supply chain partnerships develop when customers and suppliers recognise the supply chain and linkages in a value system.

9.3   The correct answers are:

- Inbound logistics
- Marketing and sales
- Service

The other primary activities are operations and outbound logistics.

9.4   The correct answer is: Suppliers, manufacturers, distribution channels and customers' value chains.

Porter's value system reflects the importance of adding value at all stages in the supply chain – from the first supplier in the chain to the end user or customer.

9.5   The correct answer is: Sheila.

Steve is in firm infrastructure.

Sunny is in procurement.

Sam is in technology development.

These are all support activities.

Sheila is in after sales service – a primary activity.

9.6   The correct answer is: 99.999%

Six sigma indicates 99.999% of manufactured items are within specification

9.7   The correct answer is: Service.

Primary activities are those across the base of the value chain – the supporting or secondary activities being shown above these. The last primary activity is supporting products sold, that is service.

9.8   The correct answer is: A number of different companies.

A supply chain is an interconnecting group of organisations which relate to each other through linkages between different processes and activities involved in producing products/services to the ultimate consumer.

9.9   The correct answer is: Comparison of a service, practice or process against one or more similar activities.

Although the other options involve some form of comparison, they do not imply comparison against similar activities.

9.10   The correct answer is: A primary activity that refers to receipt, storage and inward distribution of raw materials.

According to Porter's value chain, inbound logistics is a primary activity that refers to receipt, storage and inward distribution of raw materials.

9.11   The correct answer is: Single, multiple, delegated and parallel.

Sourcing strategies can be to use single, multiple, delegated or parallel suppliers.

9.12   The correct answer is: Products are developed in response to market signals.

In a demand network, products are 'pulled' into existence in response to demand signals.

9.13   The correct answer is: Velocity

Velocity relates to the 4 V's of big data.

The missing element of the analysis in the list above is variation in demand.

9.14   The correct answer is: Quality circles.

Quality circles are meetings of invited employees from different sections of an organisation, to discuss quality issues and hopefully agree on ideas for improvements. Empowerment is another aspect of employee participation and involvement, but is concerned with giving decision-making powers to employees.

9.15   The correct answer is: Process downtime level

Process downtime level measures the proportion of time that a process was actually running compared to what was planned.

9.16   The correct answer is: Operations management practices of structurise, systematise, sanitise, standardise and self-discipline.

The 5-S model describes operations management practices of structurise, systematise, sanitise, standardise and self-discipline. It does not describe internal analysis or a form of six sigma.

9.17   The correct answer is: 180 degree feedback.

180 degree feedback is a form of feedback on personal performance.

9.18   The correct answer is: A framework for bringing about quality improvement to a process or system.

Plan-Do-Check-Act (PDCA) was developed as an approach for improving the quality of a process or system.

9.19   The correct answer is: Reduce production bottlenecks.

Optimised production technologies focuses on the removal of production bottlenecks.

9.20   The correct answer is: Eliminate the costs of poor quality.

TQM aims to eliminate the costs of poor quality – not just reduce them. It is not possible to eliminate all quality-related costs without ceasing production. TQM does not aim to reduce the workforce – although changes in working methods may be required to improve quality.

9.21   The correct answer is: In her current role Mimi favours a collaborative approach, in her previous role she favoured an adversarial approach

In Mimi's previous role she focused on price, this is indicative of the adversarial approach. In her current role she is looking to work with suppliers on joint product development which is indicative of a collaborative approach.

9.22   The correct answer is: Crosby

Crosby's introduced the concept of zero defects, arguing that prevention is key – the cost of prevention is usually lower than the cost to fix. He also argued that workers should be involved in quality projects, and should be motivated to do something about quality.

Cousins described the strategic supply wheel. Deming favoured continual improvements via worker engagement and training. Juran drew on the Pareto principle, arguing that 85% of quality issues derive from systems weaknesses rather than worker carelessness.

9.23   The correct answer is: Increased bureaucracy.

Process redesign is typically undertaken to reduce bureaucracy. Benefits of more streamlined processes will include increased efficiency, lower costs and increased competitiveness. These process improvements are sometimes made possible by improvements in IT.

10   The finance function and sales and marketing

10.1   The correct answer is: Product orientated.

A product oriented organisation focuses on product development and features.

10.2   The correct answer is: It is concerned with the satisfaction of customer needs over the long term.

Marketing is concerned with meeting customer needs over the long term. Sales, or selling, is concerned with immediate issues of selling the product in the short term.

10.3   The correct answer is: Transferring finished goods to intermediaries who then have the task of selling those goods to consumers.

'Push' refers to the transfer of goods to third parties – the term is used because the manufacturer 'pushes' goods on to wholesalers or similar intermediaries.

10.4   The correct answer is: Penetration pricing.

Penetration pricing is used to establish or increase market share. Skim pricing involves setting an initially high price for a product. Cost-plus involves adding a mark-up on cost. Market leader pricing involves following the price set by the dominant player in the market.

10.5   The correct answer is: Introduction, growth, shakeout, maturity, decline.

The correct stages and sequence of the product life cycle are introduction, growth, shakeout, maturity and decline.

10.6   The correct answer is: Promotion.

Promotion includes all marketing communications which let the public know about an organisation's products and services.

10.7   The correct answer is: Harvest.

The product has high market share in a market with low growth and is therefore a cash cow. A harvest strategy is most appropriate because growth is weakening. If growth was still strong then a hold strategy would have been appropriate.

Divest strategy would apply to products classed as 'Dog'.

Build strategy would be appropriate to products classed as 'Question Mark'.

10.8   The correct answer is: 'Place', one component of the marketing mix.

Distribution channels, transport, warehouse and sales outlets are examples of the 'place' component in the marketing mix. Promotion usually describes advertising and physical evidence usually describes the product's environment in a service industry. The other option is irrelevant because it refers to a service organisation – the locations in the question relate to traditional consumer goods.

10.9   The correct answers are:
• Simple and easy to use
• Draws management attention to contribution

Marginal cost plus pricing does not take market and demand conditions into account. It ignores fixed costs and therefore such costs may not be covered. Therefore, it is not certain that all costs will be covered in the long term.

10.10   The correct answer is: Customers and communication.

Effective product promotion is centered on customers and communication. The other options focus on the internal business rather than the consumers.

10.11   The correct answer is: Processes

This option is relevant to services rather than products.

10.12   The correct answer is: Setting an initially high price for a new product.

Market skimming involves setting an initially high price for a new product to take advantage of those willing to pay it.

10.13   The correct answer is: Viral marketing.

Viral marketing involves the use of pre-existing social networks to spread brand awareness or other marketing objectives.

10.14   The correct answer is: Experiential.

Primarily, Jane is attempting to create an emotional link between the target and her company.

Relationship is more interactive in nature, as is post-modern.

Although you could argue that Jane's campaign is shocking, and so guerrilla, this is usually more imaginative. The aim is to create a buzz, something that will be talked about and so carry the company's message.

10.15   The correct answer is: Big data marketing.

The definition of big data is very wide. In this case, trawling the web to use unconventional, high volume sources of data to understand customers is the clue.

If Ralph Moren was simply looking at the gender of people logging onto its own website, this would be closer to the use of a conventional customer relationship management system (CRM).

If Ralph Moren was trying to get a dialogue going with the customer, this would fit into relationship marketing.

The use of a web-page is e-marketing.

If Ralph Moren was using a message that changed depending on the inputs of the consumer, such as a game, this would fit post-modern marketing.

10.16   The correct answer is: Relationship marketing.

The maximisation of customer retention and satisfaction through two-way communication is known as relationship marketing.

Postmodern marketing is about giving the customer an experience that is customised to them. Experiential marketing involves providing the customer with an experience that creates an emotional connection between the person and the brand. E-marketing is a general term relating to all electronic marketing activities.

10.17   The correct answer is: Bounce rate

Bounce rates indicate how quickly visitors leave a webpage. High, or increasing bounce rates are indication that a website is not attractive (otherwise visitors would stay longer).

10.18   The correct answer is: Product development.

According to Ansoff, product development should be undertaken when introducing new products into an existing market. This means making sure the product will be acceptable to the market.

10.19   The correct answer is: Price discrimination.

Price discrimination involves varying the price charged to customers to either increase or reduce demand so that it matches available resources. Price skimming is a marketing technique involving charging the highest price possible. Over-booking involves booking more customers onto a service than the organisation has resources to support. Cost reduction is irrelevant.

10.20   The correct answer is: Business to business.

B2B refers to business to business marketing.

10.21   The correct answers are: Service companies deliver intangible outputs, and Service companies must overcome the issue of no storage.

The specific features of service organisations that marketing departments must pay attention to include:

- Intangible outputs – it is harder to give potential customers assurances over quality. Customer testimonials may be useful for this

- No storage – services cannot be stored, thus meeting customer needs on demand is vitally important. It is better to 'under sell and over perform'

- Heterogeneity – maintaining consistent service quality is a real challenge in the absence of standardised process that can be employed by manufacturers. Extra care must be taken with training and development.

- Inseparability – as the product cannot be separated from the service delivery it is vital that service quality is maintained at all times

- No transfer of property – as there is nothing for the customer to 'hold' it can be hard to sell the benefits of the service they are buying. This can be overcome to a degree by using tools such as certificates or awards.

10.22   The correct answer is: Empty nest (i)

Consumers in this group are generally satisfied with their financial situation, and typical purchases made include travel, luxuries, home improvements.

11   The finance function and human resources

11.1   The correct answer is: A hierarchy of needs.

Maslow's theory of motivation describes a hierarchy of needs from physical needs up to self-actualisation.

11.2   The correct answer is: If targets are not met then employees may become demotivated.

The main risk of performance related pay is demotivation. The other problems can either be overcome or are simply not relevant to PRP.

11.3   The correct answer is: Advertising copy.

Assessment centres, interviews and psychometric testing are used in the selection process.

Advertising copy is part of advertising a vacancy and is therefore part of the recruitment process.

11.4   The correct answer is: A valence.

According to Victor Vroom, valence is the strength of a person's preference for a certain outcome.

11.5   The correct answer is: The psychological contract.

The set of expectations between an organisation and its employees is known as a psychological contract.

11.6   The correct answer is: The mutual expectations of an employee and employer.

This is the psychological contract.

11.7   The correct answers are:

- It saves the manager time
- Offers increased responsibility to the individual.

Subordinates tend to know their superior better than superiors know their subordinates – this is an advantage of an upward appraisal.

People are often not the best judges of their own performance – this is a disadvantage of self-appraisals.

11.8   The correct answer is: Force = Valence × Expectation.

Force = Valence × Expectation represents Victor Vroom's model of motivation.

11.9   The correct answer is: Scientific.

F W Taylor is associated with the scientific school of management thinking. These management theorists held the view that work problems can be resolved scientifically through experimentation and the analysis of the results, until an optimum solution is found.

11.10   The correct answer is: Adjustments to an individual's job content and role.

Job enlargement, enrichment and rotation are all methods of improving employee motivation by introducing changes to an individual's role.

11.11   The correct answer is: Significant influence by uncontrollable factors.

This tends to break the link between performance and reward.

11.12   The correct answer is: As part of a selection process.

An 'assessment centre' approach is used in the selection process.

11.13   The correct answer is: The movement of an individual to another post in order to gain experience.

Job rotation involves individuals moving from post to post.

11.14   The correct answer is: Performance appraisal based on feedback from peers, subordinates, line managers and even external parties.

360 degree feedback includes appraisal 'from all angles'; subordinates, peers, line managers and possibly external parties.

11.15   The correct answer is: Advertising a vacancy and initial screening of candidates.

Recruitment describes the process of attracting suitable candidates to apply for selection. Interviews and tests are part of selection.

11.16   The correct answer is: Employee churn rate.

Churn rate indicates the speed at which employees leave an organisation. High or increasing churn rates may indicate low morale and action is necessary to rectify it.

11.17   The correct answer is: A person specification.

These qualities focus on the person. A job description explains what is required in a job. The other options are part of an appraisal system.

11.18   The correct answer is: Remuneration levels.

Taylor assumed that workers are rational so would try to obtain the highest remuneration for the least effort.

Stability might seem like a desirable feature in its own right, but it is covered by substantiality.

11.19   The correct answer is: The difference between the knowledge and skills that it has and the knowledge and skills that it wants.

The training gap is the difference between the knowledge and skills that an organisation has and the knowledge and skills that the organisation wants or needs to achieve its strategy.

11.20   The correct answer is: Succession planning.

Succession planning is used by an organisation to ensure that suitable staff are available for promotion when they are needed.

11.21   The correct answer is: Compressed week.

Flexibility can be achieved in the following ways:

- Remote working – using the internet to allow employees to work from home
- Flexitime – hourly targets can be achieved in a pattern to suit workers
- Shift system – allowing staff to work outside of the 'normal' workday
- Compressed week – working fewer, longer days
- Job sharing – two employees combine to perform a full-time job between them
- Part-time – allowing staff to work a reduced number of hours

12   The finance function and IT

12.1   The correct answer is: It has a single supply chain.

A virtual company is one that is made up of a number of smaller individual entities that work on projects together. They have the benefits of a larger organisation, such as economies of scale and low cost base, but they are also able to respond to changes to the environment quickly because they do not have a rigid structure.

The lack of rigid structure means there is often more than one supply chain – depending on which entity has capacity at any point in time.

12.2   The correct answer is: Developments in technology and information systems.

Virtual teamworking is made possible by developments in communications and other technology, enabling people to work together even when they are not physically located in the same place.

12.3   The correct answer is: By changing the way in which products are made

CIM systems involve computers controlling the production process. It has therefore changed how products (not services) are made (rather than the type of products made). It is not a method of communication between organisations.

12.4   The correct answer is: Customer relationship management (CRM).

Customer relationship management systems are software applications which specialise in providing information concerning an organisation's products, services and customers.

12.5   The correct answer is: An expert system.

Expert systems allow general users to benefit from the knowledge and techniques of human experts.

12.6   The correct answer is: Measuring and analysing the existing system.

Measuring and analysing the existing system would be one of the first development activities. New buildings and wiring/air-conditioning are installation costs. Staff training is a personnel cost.

ANSWERS

12.7 The correct answer is: Digital filing systems

The other three points are examples of knowledge work systems.

12.8 The correct answer is: Decision based software.

Decision based software provides managers with the information and analysis tools to enable them to make decisions.

12.9 The correct answer is: Average age of IT infrastructure.

As hardware gets older and nearer to the end of its useful life it is more prone to breakdowns. High first call resolution indicates that the IT support team is performing well. Project costs variance is not relevant to hardware breakdowns in the near future. Security breaches relate to cyberattacks which affect software not hardware.

12.10 The correct answer is: A cookie.

Cookies are used to store information about website visitors.

12.11 The correct answer is: A database built upon past knowledge and experience.

An expert system is best described as a database built on knowledge and experience. It may not be off the shelf and does not provide help and advice – it makes decisions.

12.12 The correct answer is: Virtual organisations.

A virtual organisation, or company, is actually a collection of separate companies, each with a specific expertise, who work together to compete for bigger contracts/projects than would be possible if they worked alone. They often rely on new technology such as remote networking, the internet and extranets.

12.13 The correct answer is: Denial of service attacks.

Denial of service attacks attempt to disable an internet site by overloading it with traffic.

12.14 The correct answer is: Communication between computers within a limited geographical area.

A LAN is, by definition, used over a limited geographical area.

12.15 The correct answer is: An enterprise-wide system.

An enterprise-wide system is designed to co-ordinate all an organisation's functions, resources and information.

12.16 The correct answer is: Direct changeover.

In a direct changeover the old system is completely replaced by the new system in one move. This carries the highest risk because there is no parallel running or piloting of the new system first.

12.17 The correct answer is: Pilot operation.

Selecting one part or several parts of an organisation (eg a department or branch) to operate the new system in parallel with the existing system is known as a pilot operation.

Parallel running is used where the two systems are used by all areas of the business that will use the new system.

Phased or modular changeover is where only part of the new system is brought online at a time.

In a direct changeover the new system is switched on and the old system is switched off at the same time.

12.18 The correct answer is: Megan has created tacit knowledge.

Tacit knowledge refers to knowledge that the organisation has, but, is unaware of, or, is unable to use; for instance her new discovery which lies untapped. If this discovery is brought to light, and its significance grasped then it would become a form of explicit knowledge. Data is raw facts and figures, and information is processed, organised data that has some value.

Practice mock questions

Questions

1 **Which of the following is an example of indirect marketing?**

   ○ Writing an advertising email to send to existing customers

   ○ Targeting individual customers with promotional material

   ○ Posting 'blogs' online to draw attention to the organisation

   ○ Providing free e-books on social media sites

2 **What are the primary objectives of profit-oriented and non-profit oriented organisations?**

   ○ Profit-oriented organisation   Non-profit oriented organisation
      Output of goods/services   Minimise costs

   ○ Profit-oriented organisation   Non-profit oriented organisation
      Output of goods/services   Provision of goods/services

   ○ Profit-oriented organisation   Non-profit oriented organisation
      Maximisation of wealth   Minimise costs

   ○ Profit-oriented organisation   Non-profit oriented organisation
      Maximisation of wealth   Provision of goods/services

3 **Which of the following is a characteristic of big data?**

   ○ Value added

   ○ Variation in demand

   ○ Velocity

   ○ Visibility

4 **In terms of a feedback system, what is the name given to a measuring or recording device?**

   ○ Comparator

   ○ Sensor

   ○ Effector

   ○ Higher-level controller

5 **Data wrangling is a process used in:**

   ○ Data analysis

   ○ Data connection

   ○ Data cleansing

   ○ Data communication

6   Insights into how business functions act in compliance with rules and procedures to prevent and detect fraud would be provided by:

○   The financial reporting team
○   The treasury team
○   The internal audit team
○   The management accounting team

7   Duplicate data held in a system is also known as:

○   Corrupt data
○   Redundant data
○   Out of date data
○   Unstable data

8   Which of the following is an advantage of a functional structure?

○   Horizontal co-ordination is easy
○   Hierarchy overload will not occur
○   Good levels of communication between different functions
○   Expertise is pooled

9   Which of the following are part of the marketing mix?

Select all that apply.

☐   Product
☐   Promotion
☐   Price
☐   Strategy
☐   Production
☐   Tactics

10   In terms of the transformation process model, which TWO of the following are transforming inputs?

☐   Materials
☐   Information
☐   Labour
☐   Facilities
☐   Customers

11   Which of the following is an essential feature of a written code of ethics?

○   It states the company values
○   It is publically available
○   It rewards noncompliance
○   It's legally enforceable

12   **Which of the following is NOT an intended feature of a virtual company model?**

  ○   Improved flexibility and speed of operation

  ○   The suppliers and resources are also available to rival operations

  ○   Low investment in assets and hence less risk involved

  ○   Injection of market forces into all the linkages in the value chain

13   **Which of the following insights would be provided by the treasury team?**

  ○   Analysis of the impact of a change in accounting standards on the financial statements

  ○   Predictions of future interest rates

  ○   Quantifying key business risks

  ○   Predictions and forecasts for business performance

14   **Which of the following statements concerning cloud computing is NOT correct?**

  ○   Cloud computing shifts the bulk of IT costs from operating costs to capital costs

  ○   Cloud computing can be provided on a public or private basis

  ○   The service is fully managed by the provider

  ○   Cloud computing allows for expansion or reduction in service as the user requires

15   **Which of the following normally represents the biggest challenge in reaping the benefits of centralised business support services, such as finance and IT?**

  ○   Setting up an effective shared service level agreement

  ○   Achieving reduced premises and other overhead costs

  ○   Knowledge sharing to improve quality of the service provided

  ○   Consistent management of business data

16   Magic Co operates a factory in the furniture industry. Recently, it compared the performance of its assembly team against an assembly team in the motor industry.

  Which type of benchmarking did Magic Co perform?

  ○   Internal

  ○   Strategic

  ○   Competitive

  ○   Inter-industry

17   Stakeholders are mostly interested in the success of the business, and this creates a common goal. However, in certain circumstances, stakeholder interests may create conflicts with other stakeholder groups.

Which THREE of the following are examples of stakeholder interests being aligned?

☐   Shareholders demanding rising profits and customers wanting higher quality products

☐   The company operates a share save scheme where employees become shareholders in the company

☐   Suppliers work in collaboration with the business on new product design to meet customer demands for product improvement

☐   The community wanting minimal environmental impact from the organisation disposing waste but shareholders wanting the least costly option chosen

☐   Directors may recommend that the business is taken over by another but shareholders want to remain independent

☐   Directors introduce a corporate social responsibility charter which increases the company's involvement in the local community

---

18   **CIMA's Ethical Guidelines make it clear that individuals must do which TWO of the following?**

☐   Ensure consistency is upheld in operating practices

☐   Base decision making on the primary stakeholder affected by the decision

☐   Uphold the good standing and reputation of the profession

☐   Report their organisation if it fails to following its accounting policies

☐   Refrain from any conduct which might discredit the profession

---

19   **A control system which forecasts differences between actual and planned outcomes and implements actions after the event to avoid such differences is known as:**

○   Feedback

○   Feedforward

○   Open loop

○   Activity based control

---

20   **In a feedback system, who acts on the comparison at a strategic level within the organisation by issuing new instructions in regards to inputs?**

○   Effector

○   Higher-level controller

○   Sensor

○   Manager

---

21   Which of the following statements concerning six sigma is NOT correct?

○   It is operations oriented

○   It aims to identify the root causes of errors and defects

○   It aims to produce near-perfect products and services

○   It should improve profitability

22   Which of the following is associated with the monitoring level of data analysis?

○   Database query and search tools

○   Online Analytical Processing (OLAP) tools

○   Dashboards and scorecards

○   Predictive analytics

23   Though mostly discussed in relation to quoted companies, governance is an issue for all organisations.

Which **THREE** of the following have been highlighted as risks or problems that can arise in organisations' systems of governance?

☐   Lack of dominance by a single senior executive

☐   Irregular board meetings

☐   Audit committee comprised entirely of non-executive directors

☐   Lack of employee supervision

☐   Segregation of key roles

☐   Director bonus schemes based on company performance such as profitability

24   Which of the following describes tax evasion?

○   Using tax law to your advantage to reduce the amount of tax payable

○   Moving a business overseas to avoid future tax liabilities

○   Reducing tax liability through conduct that does not frustrate the intentions of Parliament when the relevant tax law was created

○   Reducing tax liability by breaking the law

25   Which of the following tasks are NOT normally related with the internal audit function?

Select all that apply.

☐   Financial ratio analysis

☐   Effective taxation administration

☐   Managing the data used by management to identify risks

☐   Identifying methods for prioritising and managing risks

☐   Reporting on how effective risk management controls are

☐   Reporting on variances between the expected and actual financial results

BPP LEARNING MEDIA

26   Relocating a department to another country to take advantage of cost savings related to lower labour or infrastructure costs is known as which of the following?

○   Outsourcing

○   Offshoring

○   Near-shoring

○   Franchising

27   Which type of data visualisation is often used to show trend analysis?

○   Waterfall charts

○   Dashboards

○   Line charts

○   Tables

28   There are many different bases for segmentation.

Which THREE of the following might be valid for segmentation of industrial and commercial customers?

☐   Level of income

☐   Demographic

☐   Location

☐   Socioeconomic

☐   Ordering characteristics

☐   Expectations

29   Which of the following is NOT an individual right under the Data Protection Act 2018?

○   Access

○   Rectification

○   Accuracy

○   To be informed

30   From a corporate governance perspective, which of the following is the key difference between large companies quoted on the stock exchange compared with a smaller, owner-managed company?

○   Poor cash flow management

○   Ineffective management reporting

○   Emphasis on short-term profitability

○   The agency problem

31 **Which of the following is the key feature of a sales orientation that differentiates the organisation from one with a marketing orientation?**

○ Focus on satisfying customer needs and wants

○ Assumption that the customer can be persuaded to purchase given the right information

○ Assumption that customers make buying decisions

○ Collection and dissemination of customer information throughout the business

○ Strategic and day to day decisions are made interdepartmentally

32 **Time, quality and cost are the focus of which area of work for finance staff?**

○ Financial planning and analysis

○ Project appraisal

○ Taxation

○ Project management

33 **Which method of system changeover has the lowest cost?**

○ Parallel running

○ Pilot operation

○ Direct changeover

○ Phased or modular changeover

34 **Which type of technology is a smartmeter an example of?**

○ Artificial intelligence

○ Internet of things

○ Distributed ledger technology

○ Mobile technology

35 **Duplication of tasks is least likely to occur in which of the following organisational structures?**

○ Transitional

○ Project

○ Matrix

○ Functional

36 **A flat organisation is characterised by which of the following features:**

○ Narrow control spans

○ A large number of steps on the promotional ladders

○ More opportunity for delegation

○ Slow decision making and responses

37 **In terms of the attributes of the finance team, technical expertise is known as:**

○ Experience

○ Skills

○ Knowledge

○ Leadership

38 The automatic download of bank statements is an example of how technology has affected the finance function.

Which type activity is this an example of?

○ Machine-only activity

○ Human-only activity

○ Human hybrid activity

○ Machine hybrid technology

39 **Which TWO of the following are benefits of quality circles?**

☐ Employee involvement improves morale

☐ Solutions are practical and effective

☐ A guarantee of product quality, so the board no longer has to concern itself with quality issues

☐ Being able to deal with any issues thanks to a complete range of skills and experiences within the circle

☐ The scope of influence can be very wide

40 **Which of the following is NOT a key aspect of a digital mindset?**

○ Working in a creative way

○ Lifelong learning

○ Dealing with a predictable environment

○ Working in an agile way

41 Mintzberg believes that all organisations can be analysed into five components, according to how they relate to the work of the organisation and how they prefer to co-ordinate.

What is the function of the techno structure?

○ People directly involved in the process of obtaining inputs, and converting them into outputs

○ Ancillary services such as IT

○ Converts the desires of the strategic apex into the work done by the operating core

○ Analysers determine the best way of doing a job

○ Ensures the organisation follows its mission

42 Knowledge work systems (KWS) help knowledge workers create new knowledge and expertise.

Which of the following is NOT an example of a KWS?

- ○ Digital filing systems
- ○ Computer aided design (CAD)
- ○ Computer aided manufacturing (CAM)
- ○ Specialised financial software that analyses trading situations

---

43 **Which KPI for the operations function indicates how well costs are being managed?**

- ○ Capacity utilisation rate
- ○ Operating expense ratio
- ○ Order fulfilment cycle time
- ○ Rework level

---

44 **In terms of effective communication, the intended recipient of a communication is known as:**

- ○ User
- ○ Target
- ○ Stakeholder
- ○ Audience

---

45 The product life cycle considers five phases of a product life cycle.

Which THREE of the following are phases of the product life cycle?

- ☐ Maturity
- ☐ Decline
- ☐ Fall-out
- ☐ Growth
- ☐ Development
- ☐ Re-build

---

46 **Which of the following is associated with financial accounting and reporting?**

- ○ Cash management
- ○ Managing financial risks
- ○ Raising finance
- ○ Asset control

BPP LEARNING MEDIA

47 **Selection techniques need to be which TWO of the following:**

- ☐ Reliable
- ☐ 100% consistent in generating results
- ☐ Cheap
- ☐ Fair to all candidates
- ☐ Non-discriminatory against any candidates

---

48 Revenue per employee is a KPI for the HR function.

What does this KPI measure?

- ○ How satisfied employees are with their job
- ○ How quickly employees leave the organisation
- ○ How productive employees are
- ○ How competitive employee salaries are compared to other organisations

---

49 **Which of the following is an improvement to information for decision making that results from process automation?**

- ○ It increases the range of information available to decision makers
- ○ It allows fast assembly of prototype products
- ○ It eliminates errors and inconsistencies in data that result from human inputting
- ○ It allows information to be streamed in real time

---

50 **Which novel technology impacts on how insights are communicated?**

- ○ Data visualisation
- ○ Data analytics
- ○ Mobile technology
- ○ Cloud computing

---

51 **Which of the following is an advantage of a one-to-one recruitment and selection interview?**

- ○ Can allow a rapport to build
- ○ A general judgement can be based on a single attribute
- ○ Involving more than one interviewer could result in differing opinions
- ○ Interviewers can change the behaviour of the applicant through the wording of questions or non-verbal clues.

---

52 **In an ETL system, what happens at the extract stage?**

- ○ Data is converted into another form so it can be placed into another database
- ○ A back-up copy of the data is copied into cloud storage
- ○ The specified source is read and the required data removed ready for processing
- ○ Processed data is analysed to identify patterns and trends

---

53   **Which of the following is a DISADVANTAGE of performance related pay?**

    ○   It motivates employees to improve their performance

    ○   It requires close monitoring of relationships and performance and therefore has a cost

    ○   It rewards good performance

    ○   Not all employees receive the same pay rise

54   **Which of the following is a source of customer data?**

    ○   Electronic data interchange systems

    ○   Logistics systems

    ○   Relationship management software

    ○   Material requirement planning systems

55   **Which of the following is NOT a type of psychological contract?**

    ○   Co-operative

    ○   Coercive

    ○   Calculative

    ○   Co-optation

56   **Which of the following statements concerning the fourth industrial revolution is correct?**

    ○   The revolution is disrupting specific industries in a few specific countries

    ○   The revolution is limited in scope, with most industries unaffected

    ○   The revolution is blurring the lines between physical, digital and biological spheres

    ○   The revolution is at the same velocity as the third industrial revolution

57   **Which of the following is a system that enables a business to manage its relationships centrally through the storage of existing and potential customer contact information, accounts and leads?**

    ○   Customer relationship management system

    ○   Expert system

    ○   E-commerce

    ○   Cloud computing

58   **Which of the following is NOT a digital asset?**

    ○   A PDF book

    ○   An MP4 music file

    ○   A patent

    ○   A JPG picture file

59   **Which of the following statements regarding the Data Protection Act 2018 is correct?**

     ○   Individuals have a right to challenge automatic decisions made about them

     ○   Organisations can store data in any form, regardless of how hard it would be to transfer the data to other parties

     ○   Individuals must request access to information held about them in writing only

     ○   Organisations may refuse a request to stop processing information held about an individual for marketing purposes if they have a compelling reason to do so.

60   **Which type of data analysis involves finding new relationships or features in a data set?**

     ○   Confirmatory data analysis

     ○   Predictive data analysis

     ○   Exploratory data analysis

     ○   Text data analysis

Practice mock answers

Answers

1   The correct answer is: Posting 'blogs' online to draw attention to the organisation.

A common example is food magazines including 'advertising features' in the form of recipes which use a particular producer's products.

Targeting individual customers with promotional material and emails is a form of direct marketing because there are no other parties between the seller and the customer.

Providing free e-books on social media sites is a form of viral marketing because it relies on the use of pre-existing social networks to spread brand awareness or other marketing objectives by attracting attention with a free product or service.

2   The correct answer is:

Profit-oriented organisation   Non-profit oriented organisation
Maximisation of wealth   Provision of goods/services

The objective of profit-making organisations is to generate wealth for the owners. Not for profit organisations have the objective of providing goods and services (such as health and education).

3   The correct answer is: Velocity.

Velocity refers to the speed at which 'real time' data is being streamed into the organisation. To make data meaningful it needs to be processed in a reasonable time frame.

Variation in demand and visibility are features of the Four Vs of operation, used to analyse the differences between transformational processes.

Value added refers to organisational activities that add value to the customers and therefore reduce the threat of substitutes.

4   The correct answer is: Sensor.

In a feedback system, a sensor is a measuring or recording device.

5   The correct answer is: Data cleansing.

Data wrangling involves concerting raw data from one form into another to use in a different system. It is used in data cleansing.

6   The correct answer is: The internal audit team.

Insights into compliance with the organisation's rules and procedures would be provided by the internal audit team.

7   The correct answer is: Redundant data.

Data redundancy, or redundant data, is data that is duplicated within a system.

8   The correct answer is: Expertise is pooled.

Horizontal co-ordination across the functions is often impeded by the vertical barriers to information and workflow created by functional structures. It is not easy in a functional structure.

Hierarchy overload can occur because it is caused by the vertical hierarchy of a functional structure becoming isolated, with decisions piling up as top managers lack effective means of co-ordination across specialist functions.

A good level of communication between different functions is hindered, with each function often having their own jargon.

9   The correct answers are:

- Product
- Promotion
- Price

Product, Promotion and Price are three of the 4Ps of the marketing mix.

10   The correct answers are:

- Labour
- Facilities

These are transforming inputs. The other options are transformed inputs.

11   The correct answer is: It is publically available.

Whilst the code of ethics is generally aimed at and used by the company employees, to be effective it needs to be available to anybody with an interest in the company's activities and the way it does business. This will help ensure that the company and its employees are operating in line with the values and principles set out in the code of ethics across all business and community activities.

A number of factors, including the company values, may be considered when determining whether something is ethically right or wrong. This does not mean that the company values need to be part of the written code of ethics.

Compliance should be rewarded, not non-compliance.

Ethical principles are not necessarily enforced by law, although the law incorporates moral judgements.

12   The correct answer is: The suppliers and resources are also available to rival operations.

This is a disadvantage of the virtual organisation as the company cannot gain a competitive advantage by securing supply or resources solely for their use and therefore their competitors also have access to them.

Improved flexibility and speed of operation, low investment in assets and hence less risk involved and injection of market forces into all the linkages in the value chain are all advantages of virtual operations.

13   The correct answer is: Predictions of future interest rates.

The treasury team would be interested in interest rates and foreign exchange rates. The impact of a change to accounting standards would be provided by the financial reporting team. Quantification of key business risks would come under the role of the internal audit team. Predictions and forecasts with regard to business performance would be performed by the management accounting team.

14   The correct answer is: Cloud computing shifts the bulk of IT costs from operating costs to capital costs.

With cloud computing the opposite is true. The investment in capital equipment is made by the service provider, the user is just charged an operating expense.

15   The correct answer is: Setting up an effective shared service level agreement.

Setting up an effective shared service level agreement is one of the biggest challenges as the use of the shared service centres is mandatory, with the scope of resources of the business unit being reduced yet they are still accountable for the same business performance.

Shared service centres aim to achieve significant cost reductions while improving service levels through the use of standardised technology and processes and service level agreements.

16   The correct answer is: Inter-industry.

Inter-industry benchmarking involves comparing performance against the best functional area in another industry.

17   The correct answers are:

- The company operates a share save scheme where employees become shareholders in the company
- Suppliers work in collaboration with the business on new product design to meet customer demands for product improvement
- Directors introduce a corporate social responsibility charter which increases the company's involvement in the local community

Company share save schemes mean that the existing shareholders and the employees (new/future shareholders) have a common interest in the success and growth of the business.

Collaborating on product design meets the needs of the customer, ensures future sales for the supplier (and potentially increases sales if the new product improves sales growth) and the company makes more sales (and possibly more profitable sales) which provides for higher dividends for shareholders.

Introducing a social responsibility charter directly benefits the local community and may benefit employees wanting to have more involvement in community events. It could be used in marketing campaigns to increase the customer base and therefore improve profitability which benefits shareholders.

18   The correct answers are:

- Uphold the good standing and reputation of the profession
- Refrain from any conduct which might discredit the profession.

The highest standards of conduct and integrity should be observed.

Ensure consistency is upheld in operating practices – just because a task has always been performed in a certain way does not mean that it is an ethical practice and this should be challenged when encountered by a CIMA member.

Base decision making on the primary stakeholder affected by the decision – pressure from supervisors, friends and relatives or key stakeholders can be a difficult conflict to be managed by a CIMA member and should be referred up the organisation's hierarchy or CIMA can be consulted for the ethical course of action.

There is no requirement to report an organisation for failing to follow its accounting policies. There may be legitimate reasons for doing so.

19   The correct answer is: Feedback.

Feedforward control systems use forecast, rather than historic, results to take action during the financial period.

An open loop control system does not observe the output of the process it is controlling and focuses only on the current state and its model of the system.

Activity based control systems are based on the activity-based costing methodology.

20   The correct answer is: Higher-level controller.

In a feedback system, both the effector and higher-level controller acts on the comparison, but it is the higher-level controller that does so at a strategic, or more senior, level within the organisation.

21   The correct answer is: It is operations oriented.

Six sigma is customer focused rather than operations oriented. By improving customer satisfaction, profitability should increase. The other options are correct statements.

BPP
LEARNING
MEDIA

22   The correct answer is: Dashboards and scorecards.

Scorecards and dashboards provide a window into what is happening now, the subject of the monitoring level of data analysis.

Database query and search tools are associated with the reporting level, OLAP tools are associated with the analysis level and predictive analytics are associated with the prediction level.

23   The correct answers are:

- Irregular board meetings
- Lack of employee supervision
- Director bonus schemes based on company performance such as profitability

These have all been instrumental in past high profile corporate scandals and collapses.

24   The correct answer is: Reducing tax liability by breaking the law.

Tax evasion is illegal and involves reducing tax liability by breaking the law. For example, by deliberately understanding profits.

Tax avoidance involves using tax law to your advantage to reduce the amount of tax payable. It is legal, but less than ethical because it involves applying the law in a way that it was not intended to be applied.

Tax mitigation involves reducing tax liability through conduct that does not frustrate the intentions of Parliament when the law was created.

Moving a business overseas to avoid a tax liability may come under tax avoidance or mitigation depending on the circumstances.

25   The correct answers are:

- Financial ratio analysis
- Effective taxation administration
- Reporting on variances between the expected and actual financial results

Financial ratio analysis is part of the financial accounting function.

Effective taxation administration is part of the treasury function.

Reporting on variances between the expected and actual financial results is part of the management accounting function.

26   The correct answer is: Offshoring.

Is the relocation of some part of an organisation's activities to another country.

Near-shoring is a form of offshoring but the department is relocated to a country within the region of the business.

Outsourcing involves an organisation sub-contracting its business activities to external providers who may be in the same country as the organisation, or based overseas.

Franchising is the setting up of a licensing agreement for other companies to sell the franchisor's products or provide their services.

27   The correct answer is: Line charts.

Line charts are used to show trend analysis, or other time-based results (such as sales over the last five years).

28   The correct answers are:

- Location
- Ordering characteristics
- Expectations

Level of income, demographic and socio-economic could all be suitable bases to segment consumer markets based on individuals.

29   The correct answer is: Accuracy.

      Accuracy is a principle of the Data Protection Act 2018. The other options are rights
      granted under the Act.

30   The correct answer is: The agency problem.

      This is caused by the shareholders not having access to the day-to-day company
      management information and therefore having to rely on the directors to act in their
      interest.

      Emphasis on short-term results can lead to the concealment of problems or errors, or
      manipulation of accounts to achieve desired results in large organisations. In small owner-
      managed organisations it may risk the longevity of the enterprise.

      Poor cash flow management and ineffective management reporting can occur in
      organisations of any size and management structure.

31   The correct answer is: Assumption that the customer can be persuaded to purchase given
      the right information.

      A sales orientation looks inward at the business and its need to sell products or services.
      The assumption is that customers are reluctant to purchase but that a good sales force can
      sell just about anything to anybody.

32   The correct answer is: Project management.

      Time, quality and cost are key considerations of project management. The objective of
      this area is to ensure projects are delivered on time, to the correct quality and within
      budget.

33   The correct answer is: Direct changeover.

      Direct changeover is the cheapest because it is also the quickest and most straightforward.
      There is no trial period or dual running of systems. The old system is simply switched off
      and the new system is switched on.

34   The correct answer is: Internet of things.

      The internet of things consists of computing devices, objects and mechanical and digital
      machines which can transfer data over the internet without requiring human-to-human or
      human-to-computer interaction. Smartmeters are part of the internet of things because
      they can autonomously send and receive data over the internet without human interaction
      (such as automatic meter readings).

35   The correct answer is: Functional.

      In a function structure expertise is pooled into specialist areas which avoids duplication and
      enables economies of scale.

      The other three structures all have potential for duplication to be introduced.

36   The correct answer is: More opportunity for delegation.

      All the other points are features of a tall organisation.

37   The correct answer is: Knowledge.

      Knowledge refers to the technical expertise that members of the finance team have. Skills is
      the ability to apply the knowledge and experience is the overall mastery of a particular
      area. Leadership is separate to technical expertise.

38   The correct answer is: Machine-only activity.

      A machine-only activity is a routine transaction (such as the automatic download of a bank
      statement) to which the only human input would be to correct errors or inconsistencies.

39   The correct answers are:

- Employee involvement improves morale, (because the employees feel empowered and their contribution valued).

- Solutions are practical and likely to be effective, (because workers know the processes involved).

Disadvantages:

In some cases, members of quality circles address issues that they do not possess the necessary skills to address, and management may not be aware that resolving a problem will require a consultant with special expertise. As a result, the team may waste valuable time as it continues to rely on the skills of the QC group to solve the problem.

The scope of influence can become very wide and it can be difficult to control employee power.

Quality circles help to improve, but do not guarantee quality. The board still has to concern itself with quality issues.

40   The correct answer is: Dealing with a predictable environment.

The digital environment is unpredictable and dynamic, hence the importance in being able to deal with uncertainty.

The other options are key aspects of the digital mindset.

41   The correct answer is: Analysers determine the best way of doing a job.

People directly involved in the process of obtaining inputs, and converting them into outputs – Operating core

Ancillary services such as IT – Support staff

Converts the desires of the strategic apex into the work done by the operating core – Middle Line

Ensures the organisation follows its mission – Strategic Apex

42   The correct answer is: Digital filing systems.

These are an example of an office automation system (OAS).

43   The correct answer is: Operating expense ratio.

The operating expense ratio compares operating expenses (costs) to sales revenue and is an indication of how well costs are being managed compared to revenue.

44   The correct answer is: Audience.

Effective communication is based on three factors, audience, frequency and format. The recipient might be a stakeholder, but in communication terms they are the audience.

45   The correct answers are:

- Growth
- Maturity
- Decline

The other phases are introduction and shakeout.

46   The correct answer is: Asset control.

The other points are associated with treasury management.

47   The correct answers are:

- • Reliable
- • Fair to all candidates

While selection techniques strive towards consistency, it is impossible to have one which generates 100% consistent results.

While selection techniques should be cost-effective, those that generate high benefits may incur high costs.

Selection techniques are designed to discriminate against those candidates that are less suitable for the role.

48   The correct answer is: How productive employees are.

Revenue per employee is a measure of productivity. How quickly employees leave is the churn rate, employee satisfaction is measured by a satisfaction index and how competitive salaries is measured by a salary competitiveness ratio.

49   The correct answer is: It eliminates errors and inconsistencies in data that result from human inputting.

Process automation helps to eliminate errors and inconsistencies in data that result from human inputting. Increased range of information comes from the internet of things, fast assembly of prototypes comes from 3-D printing and real time streaming is an improvement from big data.

50   The correct answer is: Data visualisation.

It is data visualisation that impacts on how insights are communicated. For example, dashboards and mapping tools allow new ways of presenting information that can be drilled into for a rich variety of information.

51   The correct answer is: Can allow a rapport to build.

The role of the manager should be decreased not increased.

52   The correct answer is: The specified source is read and the required data removed ready for processing.

The extract stage is the first stage of an ETL system. Data is read from the specified source and material required to be transformed is extracted.

At some stage, a backup is likely to be taken, but this would be before the extract stage begins. The conversion of data occurs at the transform stage. Identifying patterns and trends in data just describes data analytics.

53   The correct answer is: It requires close monitoring of relationships and performance and therefore has a cost.

There is a cost implication of performance related pay against other methods of remuneration. However it links performance and reward and therefore encourages employees to act in a manner that benefits the organisation. Although not all employees receive the same pay rise, they all have the same opportunity to gain it.

54   The correct answer is: Relationship management software.

Relationship management software will hold information about customers, such as their order history and some personal information. The other options are sources of operational data.

55   The correct answer is: Co-optation.

Co-optation is a method of dealing with user resistance. This method involves the presentation of partial or misleading information to those resisting change or 'buying-off' the main individuals who are at the heart of the resistance.

Coercive contract – this is a contract in which the individual considers that they are being forced to contribute their efforts and energies involuntarily, and that the rewards they receive in return are inadequate compensation.

Calculative contract – this is a contract, accepted voluntarily by the individual, in which they expect to do their job in exchange for a readily identifiable set of rewards. With such psychological contracts, motivation can only be increased if the rewards to the individual are improved.

Co-operative contract – this is a contract in which the individual identifies themselves with the organisation and its goals, so that they actively seek to contribute further to the achievement of those goals. Motivation comes out of success at work, a sense of achievement, and self-fulfilment.

56   The correct answer is: The revolution is blurring the lines between physical, digital and biological spheres.

Technologies of the fourth industrial revolution are blurring the lines between physical, digital and biological spheres. The speed of change is faster than ever before and affecting more industries and countries than previous industrial revolutions.

57   The correct answer is: Customer relationship management system.

The key aspects of the statement is the management of relationships and customer information.

An expert system is a database that holds specialised knowledge and data and allows the user to input information for the system to interpret and provide a logical decision.

E-commerce is the term that relates to trading activity that takes advantage of online/internet functionality.

Cloud computing refers to the delivery of computing as a service rather than a product, whereby shared resources, software and information are provided to computers over a network (typically the internet).

58   The correct answer is: A patent.

Digital assets are files such as PDFs, music, video and picture files that users are granted a licence to use. A patent is an intangible asset containing a design or specification for a product.

59   The correct answer is: Individuals have a right to challenge automatic decisions made about them.

This is a key right that has been developed due to the ever increasing volume of decisions made about individuals automatically.

Organisations have to uphold the right of data portability which means it must be stored in a form which is easily transferred.

Individuals may request access to information verbally as well as in writing.

Organisations must stop processing information used for marketing purposes. They can only refuse with a compelling reason where data is processed for non-marketing purposes.

60   The correct answer is: Exploratory data analysis.

Exploratory data analysis involves finding new relationships or features in a data set. Confirmatory data analysis involves proving or disproving an hypothesis. Predictive data analysis involves making forecasts and text data analysis involves extracting and classifying data from textual sources.